Veneto

DANILO REATO

BARNES & NOBLE
BOOKS
NEW YORK

VENETO

TEXTS
Danilo Reato

GRAPHIC DESIGN
Anna Galliani

© 2002 White Star S.r.l. - Via C. Sassone, 22/24
13100 Vercelli, Italy - www.whitestar.it

This edition published by Barnes & Noble,
Inc., by arrangement with White Star S.r.l.,
2002 Barnes & Noble Books

ISBN 0-7607-3273-6
M10987654321

Printed in Italy

CONTENTS

Introduction   page   10

Venice: sea, lagoon, and history   page   16

Islands, beaches, the lagoon, and the Delta   page   50

Padua and the Brenta Riviera,
Treviso and the "Joyful Region"   page   64

Vicenza, Verona, and Lake Garda   page   90

The Dolomites and the Belluno District   page   112

Trades and traditions   page   128

1 The first act performed by Venice to cut the umbilical cord that linked it to Byzantium was to choose St. Mark the Evangelist, symbolized by a winged lion, as the city's patron saint, to replace the Byzantine cult of St. Theodore.

2-3 Venice displays its deeply iridescent nature under different kinds of light, but by night, under the pale glow of the street lamps, the Doge's Palace is profoundly disquieting, as all the phantoms of its glorious past seem to be awakened.

4-5 The fertile hills of the "Joyful Region" of Treviso pour out rivers of frothy, sparkling Prosecco, one of the most popular Veneto wines, produced by the cultivation of carefully chosen types of vines.

6-7 The impressive scenery of Mounts Sorapis and Antelao constitutes a worthy backdrop to the magnificent Ampezzo Valley, where Cortina, one of the oldest and most famous mountain resorts in Veneto, is situated.

8 Verona, the proud medieval capital of the Ghibellini, which gave shelter to the exiled Dante and was the literary home of star-crossed lovers Romeo and Juliet, is encircled by a loop of the River Adige, which flows placidly between the plain and the Lessini Mountains.

9 The colorful houses on the isle of Burano, famous for lacemaking, welcome visitors and artists looking for peace and an inimitable palette of colors brimming with charm and history.

INTRODUCTION

The many and varied physical characteristics
of the Veneto region, which are hard to find
on such a large scale in other regions of Italy,
make it unique in the true sense of the word.
The variety of the landscape embraces
mountains, sunny green valleys, rounded shady
hills and endless plains, deep rivers and
tortuous steams, lakes with a mild climate
thanks to the maternal protection of the
mountains, and finally the sea, which the
Venetians learned to master long ago, making
huge profits from trade.

The secret of the immortal charm of this
delightful area lies in its diverse contours.
Not only is Veneto rich in tradition and history,
but nature has also been generous with its
fruits, from the proudly soaring Dolomites
with their permanently snow-capped pinnacles
to the delightful Euganean Hills, where
the mud still bears the traces of an ancient
volcano, and the hillsides slope gently down
to the shores of Lake Garda, covered with
flourishing vineyards.

The generosity of Mother Nature has been
matched by the skills of people and artists
capable of interacting with the surrounding
environment without dominating it. A good
example is provided by the buildings designed
by Andrea Palladio, one of the many great men
born in Veneto. His creations are able to bestow
the same artistic dignity on the hills and
countryside that buildings of other brilliant
men have bestowed on cities. Palladio paid his
homage to Veneto outside its towns and cities
brimming with art and culture, demonstrating
that the craft of the artist cannot detract from
the beauty of nature, but only enhance its
wonder. Palladio set a trend. His creations have
been envied and imitated all over the world.
However, as Dante put it, often "matter is deaf
to the artist's entreaties" and the raw material
which Palladio's imitators lacked ensured the
unique nature of "Happy Veneto."

The rivers Adige, Brenta, Piave, and the River Po with its ramified delta, constitute the lifeblood of the waters that nourish and fertilize Veneto's soil. This link between earth and water is even closer in the Venice lagoon. Here, man has learned how important it is to maintain a strong, healthy relationship with the environment, however hostile, even deviating rivers to prevent them from silting up. Venice certainly presents a unique case of a town that learned at an early stage to fight the land and defend itself against the devastating force of the sea, but that determination, for which it was renowned in the thousand-year-long history of the Venetian Republic, now has to battle against the insensitivity and incompetence of those who have the onerous task of defending the city. The ancient Venetians saved their land from invasion by barbarians, but have yet to settle who will save Venice from barbarous modernity.

10 top This photo shows an aerial view of Malcesine, a famous resort on the banks of Lake Garda which is visited by many German tourists following in the footsteps of Goethe.

10 bottom Veneto is also a region of magnificent mountain ranges and breathtaking views, as can be seen from this enchanting view of Mount Pelmo, whose impressive peak towers over Val Zoldana.

10-11 A delightful view of Bassano del Grappa with the famous roofed bridge over the River Brenta, designed by Palladio in 1569. The bridge, which has been destroyed and rebuilt countless times, is also famous for sad war songs inspired by the tradition and sacrifices of the Alpine troops.

12-13 *The island of St. Giorgio Maggiore, framed by the Gothic arches of the Doge's Palace, is characterized by the harmonious architectural design of Palladio, who masterfully blended art with an exceptionally beautiful natural setting.*

13 *Everyday life in Verona is symbolized by Piazza delle Erbe, where a colorful throng strolls past before the curious or oblivious gaze of the patrons sitting at the numerous café tables.*

14-15 *The dazzling splendor of the mosaics in St. Mark's Basilica invites visitors to travel back in their mind's eye to the golden days of old, when Venice acted as a bridge between East and West.*

The expression "Happy Veneto" does not mean that Veneto lacks problems. Its good-natured, unsophisticated, hospitable, hard-working inhabitants, to whom Italy owes its current wealth and surprising economic prosperity, as is universally acknowledged, gained that important distinction by virtue of immense, atavistic sacrifices, by the sweat of their brow, and the sad inheritance of the hardships of emigration, which was frequent in the nineteenth century and the early decades of the twentieth.

The region's wealth of tradition, which is still flourishing and proudly cherished, without being in the least contaminated by the ever greater temptations of the tourist market, is explained by the need to alternate hard work with well-deserved

hearts and minds of the most sensitive men and then transferred onto canvas, where the whole range of the artist's palette runs riot. Some of Titian's skies are only matched by the colors of the twilight and dawns of Cadore assimilated in childhood. Giorgione's **Tempest** reflects the true poetry of nature, immortalizing the fleeting moment when lightning rends the sky, illuminating a stretch of Veneto countryside to sinister effect. The clear, bright skies of Venice are imprinted on the memory by the precise perspectives of Canaletto's "camera obscura". Perhaps the best example of all is to be found in Turner's Venetian canvases which, with their infinitely intricate allusions, express the unique sensibility common to all great spirits.

The expression "Happy Veneto" is not a cliché, and you don't need to be sitting at a table in the Florian café, looking at one of the loveliest squares in the world, to understand the truth of this existential condition. In fact it's better to be in one of the characteristic inns that abound in the Veneto region, sitting in front of one of the scintillating, perfumed glasses of wine that constitute an invitation to hospitality and socializing. It's here that today's "enlightened travelers" stop on their

convivial recreation. The people of Veneto have fought a constant, hard battle with an environment which, though magnificent, is sometimes threatening and hostile, always ready to take back the fruits of the labor of generations. It is perhaps this struggle which has left its mark on this population, teaching them the wisdom of calm endurance, even when it means packing their bags and moving to far-reaching places, while still remaining loyal in their hearts to their tormented but no less beloved origins.

"Happy Veneto" also refers to magical, eloquent, bewitching art, delightful in its triumph of color. The region offers an unrivaled, varied range of artistic production, and this miracle manifests in the images, landscapes, and colors imprinted on the

"Grand Tour" to restore their spirits in the contemplative bliss of a pretty piazza in a Veneto town. There, amid the din of jumbled conversations, where the sound of the region's delightful singsong dialect mingles with that of the bells that toll at regular intervals during the working day, visitors begin to "rub their brains against other people's," to borrow a telling image from Montaigne.

At this point, the photographs can speak for themselves, because the magic eye of the camera not only shoots scenes mechanically, but also, through the sensitivity of the photographer, conveys moments, pathos, and laughter, human landscapes, atmospheres, and subtle enchantments that become memories and patiently wait their turn to be solemnly consecrated as history.

VENICE: SEA, LAGOON, AND HISTORY

16 top The Rialto Bridge, built between 1588 and 1591 according to a design by Antonio Da Ponte, with a single span supporting two rows of shops and three pedestrian lanes, was the only bridge connecting the opposite banks of the Grand Canal until the nineteenth century.

In his Recitativo Veneziano, *written especially for Fellini's film* Casanova, *poet Andrea Zanzotto paid homage to Venice with a play named after the city,* Regina *and* Venusia, *and portraying it as born like Aphrodite from the froth of the sea. The erotic nature of this artificial city, brought into the world by the "intelligent hands" of men, who have torn it from its natural element and built it on an unstable, fluid, living element like water, is almost palpable. The little islands of the Venetian archipelago are linked by thousands of support piles made of elm, larch, and oak from the woods of Montello, Cansiglio and Asolano, and the forests of Dalmatia. This vital reserve of wood and trees, palpitating with life, has been used to construct the body of the city, but it is also the main reason for its incredible fragility, as Venice learned the hard way when a devastating fire recently destroyed the opera house, La Fenice Theater.*

Venice is a beautiful city, but like all beautiful things it is fragile. It has a glassy, crystalline nature. Everything there is anomalous, from the shapes of its roads and canals to its curious layout, and something about this quality suggests ancestral love, the primordial origin, the fluidity of the maternal womb, and repressed Oedipus complexes. Its name and its epithets, including La Serenissima and La Dominante, all allude to a feminine nature. Venice is a city where physical contact is unavoidable. People literally bump into one another in its narrow alleyways, on the bridges crossing the canals, on the lanes along the canals, and in the conspiratorial darkness of a portico, which is perhaps why Casanova decided to be born there.

Many love affairs have been born and died in Venice. Alfred de Musset and George Sand, Lord Byron and his endless procession of concubines, Eleonora Duse and Gabriele D'Annunzio, and many other famous couples

16 center Punta della Dogana, just a stone's throw from the Baroque Chiesa della Madonna della Salute, stretches out into St. Mark's Basin, separating the Grand Canal from the Giudecca Canal.

16 bottom Giudecca Island, seen here in an aerial view, has a narrow, elongated shape, which is why it used to be called "Spinalonga" (long spine). It was once covered with vegetable gardens and vineyards, but became an industrial zone in the late nineteenth century.

16-17 A magnificent view of the quay, the Piazzetta and St. Mark's Square, with the Doge's Palace, the Basilica, and the belltower, affectionately dubbed "the landlord" by Venetians, silhouetted against the sky.

17 bottom From above, Venice looks like a gigantic fish floating on the calm waters of the lagoon. It is a veritable archipelago of islands joined by bridges and manmade surfaces, sometimes supported by a dense network of supporting piles.

18 top Statues and pigeons are predominate in the loveliest view over St. Mark's Basin, a large stretch of water, land, roofs, and sandbanks.

18 bottom The unusual nature of the colors used by artists in the Venetian Republic can only be understood by observing the gradual metamorphosis of the colors on the buildings, as demonstrated by the red brickwork of the bell tower.

18-19 Lonely gondolas moored on the quay, wait to take on hordes of tourists. These unique boats, which inspired the melodious song known as the barcarola, have acted as discreet witnesses to countless passionate love affairs.

19 top right Palazzo Contarini del Bòvolo is named after its unusual outer spiral staircase, reminiscent of a snail (bòvolo in the Venetian dialect).

19 bottom This view of the mouth of the Grand Canal shows the Baroque Chiesa della Salute in a typical winter atmosphere, with a still, leaden, overcast sky and the sun peeping out timidly from behind the clouds.

have met up here. Over the centuries, Venice has won the reputation of being the only city in the world conducive to love in public places, but it is also the place where passion, after blossoming, soon dies a tragic death. Even the names of various places bear out this theory, and many of them are ambiguous. Ponte delle Tette (Tit Bridge) suggests a lucrative business involving prostitution, which was one of the main pastimes and attractions of Renaissance Venice. There was even a catalogue, intended for the use of strangers, containing a list of the names of the "honored courtesans" and the services they offered. In another secluded spot not far away stands Ponte della Donna Onesta (Honest Woman Bridge), evidently such an unusual condition that it deserved special mention and a street sign all to itself, recorded for eternity on one of the characteristic plates known as ninzioleti (little sheets).

beauty of this city and the dualism on which it feeds and lives. From Punta della Dogana the sky turns to flame, the great dome of Chiesa della Salute is silhouetted darkly against the sky, and the clouds form creatures, monsters, and anamorphoses that are reflected in the water and reassembled into spectral shapes like apparitions, almost ghosts, as the fire spreads like a river of lava flowing suddenly out of the crater of a volcano and sweeping away all before it. The red brick of the houses in the Giudecca district turns to a deeper shade charged with color and highlights. The effect only lasts for a few minutes, but leaves the spectator amazed and enchanted, while the veil of evening falls inexorably like a slow curtain to conclude a spectacular performance. The only thing missing is the applause, but the sensation remains: by now Venice has won you over, and left its mark on you for all time.

In this real and virtual maze, where the

The prodigious sense of getting lost in this labyrinthine structure accentuates the aura of mystery that hovers over Venice, the bewitching old madam, who still wields her irresistible weapons of seduction far and wide. She is bowed down with age and history. Her wrinkles certainly show, in the cracks in the crumbling brickwork on the canal banks and in the salt deposits encrusted on the façades of the buildings, rising steeply upwards as if the water wanted to take back what man had snatched away from it centuries ago. In this interminable contest, the sea bides its time, waiting to get even. It's a perpetual game between Eros and Thanatos, Love and Death, a game repeated daily that enhances the voluptuous melancholy of Venice.

You have to see a sunset in autumn, when the red sun, like a ball of fire, drowns in the calm waters of the lagoon, to understand the

dimension of time does not exist, but disintegrates as in a dream, love is not the only thing that's ephemeral. Everything moves more slowly here. The steamboats zigzag up and down the Grand Canal at a snail's pace without ever watching the clock, for time has stood still here in Venice. We have just left behind us the ugly, squat railway station, which clashes so unpleasantly with the monumental exuberance of the Baroque façade of the Scalzi church designed by Longhena. As soon as we look right or left, the enchantment begins. There's the eighteenth-century Palazzo Labia, with its blocks of Istria stone dazzling in the sunlight, and on the other side a glimpse of the Orient, where a cavalier nineteenth-century restoration has given an artificial charm to the Turkish Warehouse. This building, on the main road of the city, demonstrates the hospitality of Venice, which allowed its most terrible enemy

to set up shop, make a home, and trade freely on Venetian soil. As we approach the Renaissance Palazzo Vendramin Calergi another page of history turns, and the harmonious notes of Richard Wagner echo in the air. Here, the great composer tragically ended his days before joining the legendary heroes of Valhalla immortalized in his music. Gothic arches embroider the façade of the noblest of the Venetian mansions, which the locals called Ca' d'Oro (House of Gold) as a perpetual sign of admiration. It has now been permanently restored to its original beauty following very careful renovation. At a loop of the canal we come to the crowded, noisy Neo-gothic Fish Market. Then you spot the most famous bridge in Venice, the Rialto, the pulsating heart of frenetic business activity in the past and tourism in the present day, with the rows of shops and colorful stalls of its markets, which are still surprisingly active in a city that is sadly losing large numbers of residents.

Across the bridge, the magic continues. Each palazzo bears the name of a famous family, which has given Doges to Venice: Dandolo, Loredan, and Grimani. The University now stands in the place where the famous Francesco Foscari once lived, and Carlo Rezzonico, who became Pope with the name of Clement XIII, lived in the Baroque Ca' Rezzonico, where one of the most magnificent museums displaying eighteenth-century works is housed. Every palazzo is a museum, and some have been converted into great exhibition centers, like Palazzo Grassi, whose collection has nothing to fear from comparison with other museums housing art of distant civilizations like those of the Phoenicians, the Celts, and the Greeks, or an immortal master of modern art like Pablo Picasso. The Gallerie dell'Accademia, which houses the best of Venetian art, with canvases by Titian, Giorgione, Veronese, Tintoretto, Guardi, and Canaletto, is a feast for the eye.

From the top of the wooden bridge of the Accademia, inevitably fated to be temporary, we look down on the other symbol of the slow pace of life in Venice, the gondola. Severe in appearance, with that dark color that evokes macabre fantasies, sinuous in its asymmetrical complexity, and designed to be balanced and steered by a single oarsman, it slowly cleaves the water, as if afraid to disturb its calm. It is the Queen of boats, built in accordance

20-21 Crossing the Grand Canal is like going back through centuries of history. The names of Doges and centuries of art are inextricably linked. For example, the Renaissance Palazzo Dolfin Manin stands close to the late Gothic Palazzo Bembo.

20 bottom left Ca' d'Oro is the most outstanding gem of Venetian Gothic architecture. It is named after the multicolored decorations on the marble, once covered with gilding. The building was last restored in 1984.

20 bottom right, Giorgio Massari, the spiritual heir of Baldassare Longhena, built Palazzo Grassi between 1749 and 1766. This classical, elegant, but cold façade is a precursor to Neoclassicism.

21 top The large ballroom of the Rezzonico family's mansion, demonstrates the megalomania of these eighteenth-century noblemen.

21 bottom The narrow, dark canals that flow into the Grand Canal give access to the luminous marvels of the Venetian palazzi.

with ancient rules and proportions jealously handed down from father to son and concealed in the squeri (boatyards), where the last master carpenters still carve the wood, meticulously following the ancient technique. The gondola remains untouched by the contagion of modernity, and in addition to its use for mere tourism, it continues to demonstrate its eternal practicality in the routes connecting the opposite banks of the Grand Canal.

Even the gondolier's movements follow a strict ritual: the oar is gently submerged with a regular splashing sound, dividing the water which immediately closes behind it. This is the magic of Venice. Venetians born and bred have been taught an important lesson: hurrying is forbidden in this city. Perhaps that's why those who were born in this paradise can never get used to the frenetic pace imposed by the mainland and the big cities. They can't wait to get home again. Here, loneliness is non-existent; all you have to do is go into the streets, and the crowd immediately swallows you up. Perhaps it's this excessive physical contact that is sometimes disturbing, or perhaps it is the uncivilized use of the city by the inappropriate "hit and run" type of tourism imposed by modern travel agencies, but in Venice it is sufficient to know your way round the streets, with Ariadne's thread as your guide.

After a few paces Venetian finds themselves with people who speak their own gentle tongue. You can smell the fragrance of the gargantuan meals prepared in homes and inns off the beaten track, where for once the patrons don't speak German, English, or French but only pure Venetian dialect, even among animals, such as stray cats, dogs, and pigeons. The old "cat lady" calls every puss by name, and each cat answers, slyly meowing and rubbing itself slowly against the old lady's hobbling legs to demonstrate its infinite gratitude. Venice is a city that loves animals. The lagoon also offers shelter to flocks of gleaming black cormorants together with the reluctant little egrets with their aristocratic reserve that perch suspiciously on the sandbanks, and there are seagulls everywhere. They swoop down into the streets and mingle with the feeding pigeons and some of them even venture timidly into the shops to beg with their impertinent screeching cry. It sometimes makes you wonder whether they don't enjoy the best view of the city. If you climb the bell tower of St. Mark's

23 bottom Procession in St. Mark's Square *by Gentile Bellini, which belongs to the* Miracle of the Cross *cycle, portrays a solemn moment in Venetian popular worship.*

("the landlord" as the Venetians familiarly call it) on a clear day, you can look out over that stretch of water, roofs, houses, and steeples and imagine you're in perpetual flight like those seagulls, the true dominators of the huge placid lagoon studded with sandbanks and islands.

How delightful it must be to fly over lanes and squares, and perch on the pinnacle of a bell tower. Bell towers abound in Venice, as do churches. Some are small and austere and others huge, like those containing the mortal remains of the Doges, such as the Gothic Church of Saints John and Paul, run by Dominican monks, or the almost twin church of Santa Maria Gloriosa dei Frari, named after the Franciscan Friars Minor. This monumental complex contains five centuries of Italian history, to which the divine brush of Titian added the marvelous Assunta altarpiece.

Now, it is time to fly off again towards St. Mark's Square. There is often too much of a crowd queuing in front of the Basilica, and too many groups of Japanese tourists staring upwards, camera or camcorder at the ready, waiting to capture the Moors that have punctually sounded the hours on the Clock Tower with their slow, precise movements for nearly 500 years. The eyes are dazzled by the mosaics, from which light reflects onto the glass of a window of the Procuratie above the iron tables of the Florian, Lavena, and Quadri cafés, while the melodies played by their orchestras linger in the air, often mingled with the slow, deafening peal of the bells trying to regain their lost musical supremacy over the Square that once belonged to them alone. The Doge's Palace awakens, but except in occasional historical pageants, we no longer hear the sound of trumpets and the roll of drums announcing the Doge's appearance at the window of his majestic palace, the seat of government, the law courts, and the Doge's residence, with Gothic arches that appear to have been designed by a skilled lace maker.

The impressiveness of the building is evident as soon as the visitor passes through the Gothic Map Gate, when its grandiose size is demonstrated and the pattern of the loggias is interrupted by the Giants' Staircase, designed by Antonio Rizzo in the late fifteenth century, with the two statues of Neptune and Mars which are clear allegories for Venetian dominion over land and sea. Not far away stands the

24-25 Venice's palazzi contain art treasures, exquisite stucco work, and elegant furnishings, as can be seen in the delightful drawing room of Palazzo Contarini-Fasan, traditionally known as "Desdemona's House." This palazzo is perhaps one of the smallest of those lining the Grand Canal, but it is easily distinguished by its single-lighted and three-lighted mullioned windows, accompanied by little balconies with a lacy openwork pattern.

24 bottom left Palazzo Pisani-Moretta owes its charm to the Late Gothic architecture, enhanced by the magnificent central double six-lighted window with its entwining quatrefoil arches.

24 bottom right Palazzo Contarini dalle Figure is named after the two figures of monsters crushed under the main balcony. However, it is interesting not so much for its Istria stone façade as for the novelty constituted by the insertion of a four-lighted window surmounted by a tympanum.

25 The Labia family, which came from Catalonia, made its fortune in trade. They spared no expense to fresco the rooms of their residence in Campo San Geremia, commissioning the work from the expert hand of Giambattista Tiepolo.

Golden Staircase by Sansovino, which abounds in cherubs and figures of women and symbolizes the magnificence of the Venetian Republic, stuccoes by Alessandro Vittoria literally drowning in gold, the Doge's Apartments and the astonishing atmosphere of the High Council Room, where the huge Paradise canvas, painted by Jacopo Tintoretto with the aid of his son Domenico and Palma the Younger, stands out on the back wall. Visitors entering the Room of the Three State Inquisitors are liable to shudder, and it does not require much imagination to do so, because a small staircase leads to the terrifying Torture Chamber where a sinister rope immediately evokes the agony that was in store for the unfortunate people who fell into disgrace.

The Bridge of Sighs, which crosses the Rio di Palazzo, fires the imagination of incurable romantics, who remember tragic stories of prisoners awaiting trial being taken to the Prisons in the fear of being left to rot forever, condemned to the terrifying damp of the pozzi (well prisons) or forced to dream of adventurous escapes from the piombi (lead prisons) if they were to avoid certain death. At the foot of Ponte della Paglia (Straw Bridge) lies the wide Riva degli Schiavoni, which commemorates sailors from Schiavonia (now Dalmatia). This panoramic route running alongside St. Mark's Basin is lined with the most famous hotels in Venetian tradition: the Danieli, the Gabrieli, and the Londra. The long road continues alongside the Parish Church of St. Zaccaria until it makes a triumphant entrance into St. Mark's Square.

Today, the only inhabitants of this past are tourists, who rush ecstatically from one route to another, dazed by the incredible variety of all this splendor. Sometimes they stop and rest in the Piazzetta, between two tall monoliths of Oriental granite that dominate the quay and

26-27 The colorful "column" or "palazzo" posts which can be seen in the foreground, often decorated with friezes and coats-of-arms, are used as mooring posts for gondolas and to mark the boundary of the waters owned by each palazzo.

27 bottom Rio di San Trovaso with Ponte delle Meravegie (Bridge of Marvels). The bridge is actually named after Palazzo Maravegia, owned by the Maravegia family, although some say it takes its name from wondrous events that occurred on that stretch of the canal.

28 top Greengrocers' shops set up in boats, like this one moored at the foot of Ponte dei Pugni at San Barnaba, are a common sight in this city that floats on the water.

St. Mark's Basin. On one column stands a winged lion, which in reality is perhaps an ancient Chinese chimera, and on the other stands the statue of St. Todaro (Theodore), a Byzantine saint and the first patron saint of the city. Here, it is easy to imagine that you are inside a painting by Guardi or Canaletto, perhaps during the Easter Thursday Festival, amid tumblers, acrobats, charlatans, and fortune-tellers. We can also meditate on the priceless treasures in the Libreria Sansoviana, designed by Jacopo Sansovino and begun in 1537 to house the precious collections, initially donated by Cardinal Bessarione. Since 1904 the library has been extensively reorganized, and is now partly housed in the neighboring rooms of Sansovino's Mint. St. Mark's National Library, with a million books, 13,000 manuscripts, many of them decorated with exquisite miniatures, and 3,000 incunabula, is a popular place of pilgrimage for book lovers from all over the world.

A group of curious souls are usually waiting patiently in front of the Loggetta to climb the bell tower, and there's no better way of passing the time than examining the reliefs, which include an interpretation of Venice in the form of Justice, an obvious allegory of good government. This was how the sculptor depicted the ideal of the perfect republic, which only Venice believed itself capable of embodying. Another huge queue usually takes root on the paving stones in front of the Basilica. The tourists are sometimes forced to stand on the rickety gangways normally used when the town center had flooded, but that have become permanent fixtures with time, and will no doubt be protected by the Historic Monuments Inspectorate sooner or later. In the meantime, they have the opportunity to learn to distinguish the mosaics, like those on the bowl-shaped vault above the main door of Sant'Alipio, among the oldest on the façade,

28 center The Rialto fruit and vegetable market, always crowded and noisy, stands next to the Neo-gothic Fish Market in a riot of color.

28 bottom In Venice it is impossible to feel lonely. You only have to go out into the streets to come into physical contact with the crowds thronging the narrow lanes.

28-29 The Rialto fish market is still the most popular meeting place for Venetians, and the whole area is crammed with stalls offering a choice selection of sea and lagoon fish.

29 bottom The exquisite gondolas are a source of wealth and income for the gondoliers, and therefore receive the kind of treatment normally lavished on custom-built sports cars on the mainland.

30 top left The terrible Venetian prisons were divided into piombi (lead prisons), named after the lead covering the roof tiles, and pozzi (well prisons) like the one seen in the photo, with small, low-ceilinged, unhealthy cells where death came as a happy release.

30 top right From the portico on the piano nobile the magnificent loggia of the Ca' d'Oro resembles a fragile spider's web which, like a lense, filters and fragments the wonderful view over the Grand Canal.

30 center At the Doge's palace, Vittore Carpaccio asserted the rule of the Venetian Republic over land and sea, depicting the symbol of the city's patron saint, the winged lion, with its front paws resting firmly on land, and its hind paws on the sea.

which include the Procession bearing S. Mark to the Basilica, or to see a replica of the gleaming bronze chariot brought to Venice from Constantinople in 1204, the original of which can be admired later in St. Mark's Museum. Waiting in line will eventually bear fruit. It is definitely worthwhile, because the mosaics in the atrium are breathtaking; the mosaic of the Creation, divided into three concentric circular bands, is particularly impressive, as are the Stories of Noah, the ark, and the great flood. The interior is a feast for the eye too, with the Pentecost and Ascension Domes and the dazzling Gold Altarpiece. Now, the Stendhal Syndrome begins to take effect.

There are often far too many people in the Square and it would be best to fly off with one of the seagulls to the island of San Giorgio, soaring over the churchyard with its geometrical, perspective paving. Then, from the roof of the classic church designed by Palladio it could swoop right into the heart of La Giudecca, which features another masterpiece by the great architect, the Church of the Redeemer, with its impressive scenic staircase. This Church was erected by the Senate as a votive offering to give thanks for the end of the terrible plague of 1576. Finally, taking flight again, allowing itself to be blown along by the

30 bottom The Golden Staircase at the Doge's Palace, which was begun in 1554 using a design by Sansovino and later continued by Scarpagnino, was so called because of the abundance of gold and white stucco decoration.

31 The Doge's Palace was the prestigious seat of government in the Venetian Republic, symbolizing its power. The Venetians also turned it into an artistic center, and it was not only the residence of the Doge, but also the headquarters of the Republic's judiciary.

agile currents and winds, the feathered master of the lagoon gazes towards the endless neat rows of vines and vegetable gardens tended by monks, far, far away.

The Lido awaits the flight of the gull with its famous beaches, magnificent Art Nouveau villas and luxury hotels, synonymous with the decadent atmosphere described by Thomas Mann, along with the wild dunes of the Alberonis. Flying back, it can observe Venice from above, as if the city were the biggest fish in the world floating on the sea, with its snaky intestines of placid water instead of bones. This watery outlet, where the workshops of the Arsenal flourished long ago, was once much more attractive, with its sailing ships, armed galleys, and sails unfurled in the wind, back in the days when the lion of Saint Mark, rampant on the glorious banner, roared and unsheathed

its claws. Now, it's milder and has adopted a "crablike" pose, as the locals put it; the lion has lost his claws and learned to feed on resignation. "What an odd city this is," wrote Jean Cocteau, "where lions fly and pigeons walk!"

This marvelous paradox is hard to understand, even for a seagull, so perhaps it's just as well to seek Venice elsewhere, above the high roofs of the very first skyscrapers in history, the Jewish homes in the Ghetto. This magnificent community had its own pawnshops and modest dwellings, together with splendid synagogues built between 1500 and the mid-seventeenth century: the German and Canton Shuls for worship in accordance with the Ashkenazi rite, the Italian Scola in accordance with the Italian rite, and the Levantine and Spanish Shuls in accordance with the Sephardic rite. Venice holds the unenviable record of having coined the terrible word ghetto, which derives from the fact that foundries (called geti in Venetian dialect) once stood in the circumscribed area assigned to the construction of residential buildings and shops. However, it must be said in its defence that the Venetian Republic was far more tolerant towards the Jewish community than many other countries, as demonstrated by the profusion of art and culture that can still be admired in the Jewish Museum.

A short distance away in the Cannaregio district lies Campo dei Mori, an odd little piazza that transports us into the midst of the Levant. Here, blood-red brick issues from niches resembling open wounds in the walls of old houses with crumbling plaster, and characters dressed in oriental costumes and wearing turbans look down on us. They're merchants, who look like something out of a play by Goldoni. Can it be the Impresario of Smyrna, or the Armenian Abagiggi from Women's Gossip, with his incomprehensible

32 This portrait of Doge Foscari kneeling before the lion, a copy of a work by Luigi Ferrari painted in 1885, is situated above the Map Gate, the majestic entrance to the Doge's Palace designed by Bartolomeo Bon. The Gate is so called because it stands near the State Map Department's depots and archives.

33 left This Late Roman porphyry group of the Tetrarchs or Moors on the surviving corner tower of the Doge's Palace is traditionally said to portray Diocletian and the other three Emperors who reigned with him.

33 top right Justice is solemnly portrayed in a Gothic bas-relief in the Doge's Palace, situated in the quatrefoil of the loggia and

attributed to Michelino da Besozzo or the Bon School.

33 center right Four Archangels are portrayed in the corner sculptures of the Doge's Palace. This photo shows the Archangel Michael above the scene of the Original Sin. The capitals and corner reliefs were intended by the clients to have a mainly educational function.

33 bottom right L'Ebrezza di Noè (The Drunkenness of Noah an allegory of indulgence), a sculpture by Lombard masters of the fourteenth/fifteenth century, stands on the corner of the Doge's Palace nearest Ponte della Paglia (Straw Bridge), with the Bridge of Sighs in the background.

Armenian dialect? Historians had great difficulty in deciphering the puzzle, and eventually agreed that the figures portray three brothers from the Mastelli family, traders from Peloponnesus who owned a palace nearby. Its bas-relief portraying an oriental merchant with a camel still surprises those who venture into these remote parts of the city.

Venice was the gateway to the East. Its merchants traveled everywhere, and in every Venetian there is a drop of the blood of these travelers of old, the best known of whom is Marco Polo. If anyone still alleges that the tales told in Polo's book Million are merely fantasies or tall stories, he should visit these places and consider the remnants of the communities scattered all over Venice, such as the Greek, Turkish, and Armenian communities which had warehouses, churche, and even islands of their own in this cosmopolitan city. Why were all these people so happy in Venice that they made it their home? Undoubtedly because in Venice they could breathe a Levantine air, an oriental magic produced by centuries of coexistence and trade, which introduced half Europe to products once rare or wholly unknown, such as purple, exquisite fabrics, hides, and above all, costly spices.

To go even further back in time, while much of Europe was united in a rigid feudal structure under Charlemagne and civilization had escaped from the Dark Ages by the skin of its teeth, these strips of islands, the mainland and the stinking, unhealthy, inhospitable marshes which formed the nascent Venice recognized Byzantium as the only true heir of ancient civilization, which was how the city came to act as a bridge between East and West. To confirm their loyalty, the Venetians used geometrical

34 top The exquisite coffered ceiling of the Senate Hall in the Doge's Palace was finely carved and decorated profusely with gold to demonstrate the power and wealth of the Venetian Republic to visitors.

34 bottom The wealth of decoration on the vault and the stuccoes depicting Victory in the Sala dell'Anticollegio enabled guests to while away the time before being received by the Doge.

34-35 The Venetian nobility, who ruled the Republic, met in the impressive High Council Room of the Doge's Palace where they sat on benches arranged lengthwise. The assembly, chaired by the Doge and the Lords, passed laws and elected the most important State officials.

35 bottom left The Lords used to receive foreign ambassadors, and Venetian ambassadors returning from their posts, in the College Room, built by Antonio Da Ponte according to a design by Palladio and decorated with canvases by Paolo Veronese on the ceiling.

35 bottom right Another prestigious antechamber in the Doge's Palace was the Hall of Four Doors, so called because of its four monumental doors. However, its greatest attraction were the frescoes on the ceiling, painted by Tintoretto according to a design by Sansovino.

tesserae of colored marble, obtained from the Byzantine provinces by robbery, piracy, or honest trade, to form mosaics on the floors of its Basilica and churches. More mosaics glittering with gold, plus enamels, Byzantine icons, precious reliquaries, perfume burners, processional lamps of fine Oriental craftsmanship, and miniatures poured into the coffers of the state and enriched the treasury of Saint Mark. That is why the Orient is ever so present in Venice.

Coming back to reality after this historical digression, prompted by the lure of a magical corner of Venice far away, composure can be regained in the monastic solitude of the Madonna dell'Orto, and admire the pretty Gothic façade in which the warm shades of the pink brickwork enhance the white marble decorations of this church, filled with works by Jacopo Robusti, known as Tintoretto, who lived in Campo dei Mori and rests in peace here. Fortunately, the noisy, intrusive tourists have not yet discovered this address. But while ordinary mortals in search of prodigies are resigned to picking their way along an endless gangway crossing the water right in the middle of the lagoon, fancifully believing that they can continue their trip as far as "glassy Murano," the seagull will leave to continue his daily patrol of the city as far as the colored houses of Burano, off towards Torcello, far, far away towards the origins of history.

36-37 St. Mark's Basilica, amazingly reminiscent of the East and Byzantium, is the symbol of this city, the Doge's chapel of the **palatium**, a place of worship, but above all a treasure trove of the arts. The majestic building, inspired by the Twelve Apostles in Constantinople, with its five domes, was consecrated in 1094, while Vitale Falier was Doge.

36 bottom left From the top of the Basilica one of the horses in the copy of the famous four-horse bronze chariot brought to Venice from Constantinople seems about to take wing over the **piazza**, which is crowded with tourists basking in the early morning sun at the tables of the famous cafés.

36 bottom right The winged lions, walking, rampant, or "crablike," which are representations of St. Mark the Evangelist, are found everywhere in the places consecrated to his legend.

37 top From the top of the clock tower, the Moors have punctually struck the hours for almost 500 years. The tower, which was built by

demolishing two arches of the Procuratie Vecchie, dates from 1499.

37 bottom The sun reflects off the mosaics of the Basilica, producing dazzling, iridescent highlights, demonstrating what Lord Byron meant when he wrote that in order to penetrate the secrets of Venice, you have to look to the Levant.

38 top The mosaics of St. Mark's cover some 86,000 square feet of the building, so that visitors can walk among the symbols of the Christian faith.

38 center The bronze four-horse chariot which was brought to Venice from Constantinople in 1204 has been lovingly restored, and is now on display in St. Mark's Museum.

38 bottom Although the exquisite mosaic decoration appears to be fragmented into a number of different legends, according to experts it actually recounts a single tale inspired by the prophetic doctrines of theologian monk Gioacchino da Fiore.

38-39 The impressive Gothic iconostasis of Pierpaolo and Iacobello Dalle Masegne, with 14 statues (the 12 Apostles, the Virgin Mary, and St. Mark) on either side of the Crucifix, stands in the nave of the Basilica.

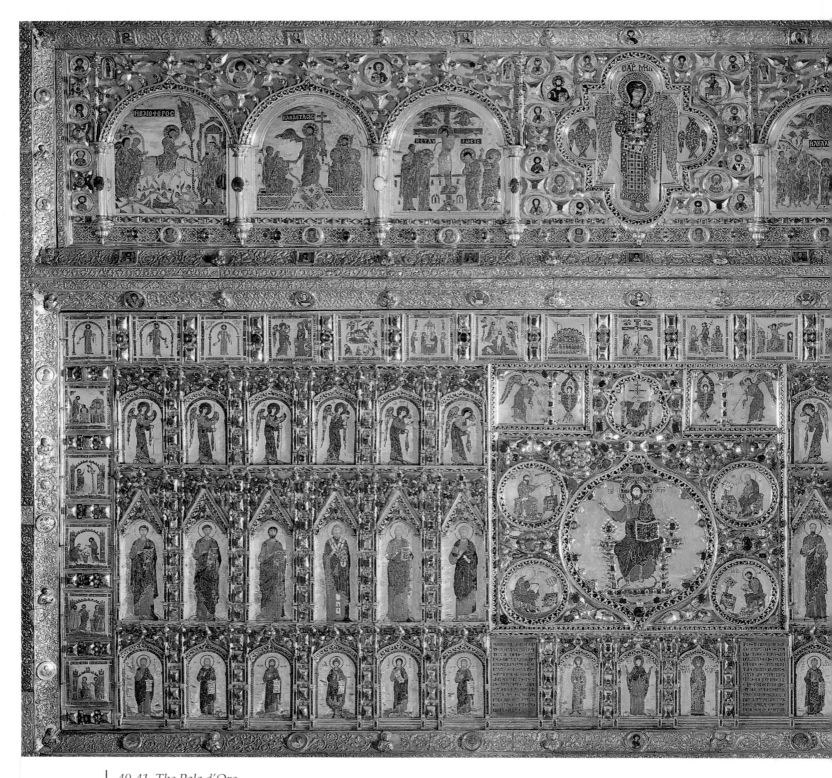

40-41 *The Pala d'Oro stands in all its glory behind the high altar of the Basilica. This gold altarpiece is a masterpiece of Byzantine and Venetian gold-work, to which goldsmith Giovanni Paolo Boninsegna added a gilded silver Gothic structure studded with rare pearls, precious stones, and enamel.*

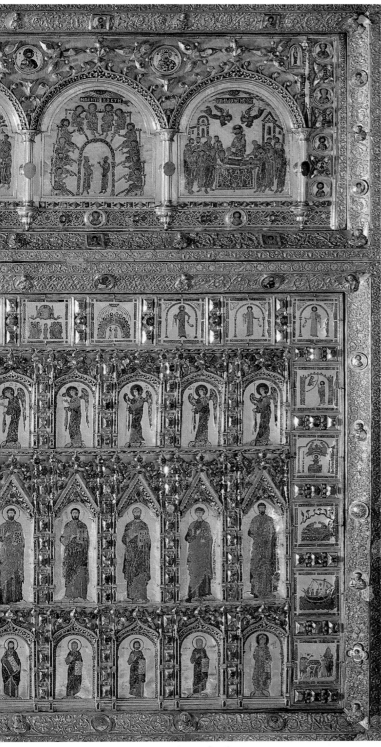

41 top The priceless silver and gilded enamel icon of the Archangel Michael, a masterpiece by eleventh-century Byzantine goldsmiths, is one of the most exquisite pieces displayed in the Treasury of St. Mark's.

41 bottom The half-length portrait of the Archangel Michael portrayed in this icon from Constantinople is another of the exquisite Byzantine gold works from the first half of the eleventh century which have always been present in St. Mark's Treasury.

40 bottom War booty and gifts flooded into Venice together with exquisite marble, especially following the sack of Constantinople. In this way, liturgical articles and reliquaries accumulated over the centuries to form one of the greatest treasures in Christendom.

42-43 *Caffé Florian, with its interiors, pretty rooms, nineteenth-century décor, and fancy decorations, including famous personalities and fanciful Oriental figures, gives a wonderful view of one of the most beautiful squares in the world.*

42 bottom *In winter Venice is shrouded in darkness at an early hour. All that remains to light the city are the characteristic street lamps with their pale light that produces a magical atmosphere, and sometimes throws sinister shadows onto the monumental buildings.*

43 top The Lavena café under the Procuratie Vecchie is known as the "musicians' café." It owes much of its fame to a famous customer, Richard Wagner, who took a table in the upper loggia every day.

43 bottom On December 29, 1720, an unknown coffee-house proprietor called Floriano Francesconi opened his café under the Procuratie Nuove, unaware that he was creating an institution.

44 top The sky is dark and threatening, the water an olive color, the roofs covered with a sprinkling of snow, and an icy north wind is *blowing, but a sudden break in the clouds allows the sun to shine through, enhancing the attractive church of St. Maria della Salute.*

44 center Dazzling white snow is in unusual contrast with the black gondolas moored, bereft of tourists, in Bacino Orseolo.

44 bottom A gondola in the snow seems to be masked, and it's no accident that it takes on the same sinister colors as the eighteenth-century Venetian "cloak and domino" costume.

44-45 Snow rarely falls in Venice, but when it does, it attracts nationwide interest. It changes the face of the city, as seen in this attractive picture that portrays Saint George Church against the background of the columns of Mark and Todaro.

45 bottom left St. Mark's Square, covered with a fine layer of snow, attracts a *crowd of onlookers who breathe the strange odor of the biting cold and look at the glistening domes of the Basilica. Only the Moors, at the top of the Clock Tower, appear to be disturbed in their centuries-old task by the color white, to which they are unaccustomed.*

45 bottom right The statue of Niccolò Tommaseo, one of the heroes of the 1848 *revolution, looks down with an austere gaze onto the huge, empty Campo di Santo Stefano on a winter's day.*

46-47 This picture of the jetty with empty gondolas evokes ancient memories, such as that of Giacomo Casanova being but a stone's throw from the Doge's Palace, ready to repeat his escape from the cells of the piombi for eternity.

48 top St. Mark's Square buzzes with life at night. The melodramatic notes of **La Traviata** *linger on the air at the Florian café, while a frenzied can-can is played at the Quadri, and the Moors wait to say goodnight to this deafening but melodious cacophany.*

48 bottom Ca' Dario, one of the palazzi *lining the Grand Canal, stands out not only for its multicolored Renaissance marble, but also for the romantically sinister curse said to afflict its owners, who have died violent deaths.*

48-49 *The blend of music played by three café orchestras turns St. Mark's Square into the loveliest ballroom in the world, where a huge virtual dome encloses the sound of music together with a babble of voices speaking every known language.*

49 bottom *Warm nocturnal shades are reflected in the trachyte paving slabs of the harbor, while a cold greenish light unnaturally illuminates the Palladian façade of the Church of St. Giorgio Maggiore.*

ISLANDS, BEACHES, THE LAGOON, AND THE DELTA

The charm of the lagoon is partly due to the incredible variability of its physical surroundings. Its colors change from one moment to the next, its clarity and its waters rise and fall according to the tides, driven by the warm sirocco winds to lap and invade the trachyte slabs that pave the streets and the Istrian stone that forms the canal banks, leaving nothing untouched, even disturbing the religious peace of the Basilica and its patron saint. The crystal-clear air after a summer cloudburst reminds us that the mountains of Veneto are not that far away, and looking towards the horizon from the Lido or the Fondamenta Nuove, sharp undulating peaks can be discerned. Taking up the oars of a boat and rowing out to Murano or even further, beyond the sandbanks, there are abandoned islands, which have housed lazarettos and important hermitages over the centuries. The mountains seem to have taken refuge on Torcello, and upon reaching that

50-51 In this delightful aerial view, Burano Island and its labyrinth of bridges and canals looks like a miniature Venice, with its numerous campielli *(little squares) and a single* piazza *named after its most famous citizen, Baldassarre Galuppi.*

50 bottom Burano is a riot of color, and its simple fishermen have inherited the magical gift of borrowing the

iridescent shades of the lagoon to paint the façades of their homes in strong hues.

51 There is an artistic atmosphere in the air at Burano, which is indeed an artists' colony. The artists who have lived there include Pio Semeghini, Filippo De Pisi, and Gino Rossi, who lived in the famous inn of Romano Barbaro.

archaically beautiful island, perhaps it will be possible to reach out as if to touch one of the many mirages that Venice so subtly distributes. The imagination runs riot in this city. It is so hard to explain that even a second book would not suffice. The secret is not to run aground on the sandbanks of rationality.

A short stretch of the lagoon separates Venice from Murano, the island where "Venetian glass" is made and that is one of the most popular destinations for tourists on package tours to

52-53 and 52 bottom
The riot of color on Burano island is manifested in numerous ways, from the gaudy hues of the boats to the amazing creativity with which characters and names are drawn on their hulls.

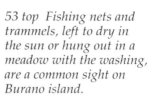

53 top Fishing nets and trammels, left to dry in the sun or hung out in a meadow with the washing, are a common sight on Burano island.

53 center In this remote corner of the lagoon, the changing highlights and rays of sunset inspire the imagination with the beauty of nature.

53 bottom In this paradise of art, even a humble bas-relief, considered almost as a family coat-of-arms by a Burano resident, acquires tone and strength, enhanced by the intense color contrast.

Venice. Its busy furnaces continually churn out all kinds of articles, from ornaments to lamps, from fragile glasses to heavy sculptures, often inspired by famous painters and designers. But Murano also offers art, great art. It's a miniature Venice, with its very own meandering Grand Canal overlooked by houses, factories, and a few palazzi which, apart from the ravages of time, still display the glories of their magnificent past, and also convey the impression that the island's prosperity began at a very early date. The magnificent church of Saints Mary and Donato, one of the most characteristic examples of Veneto-Byzantine style, was built by the descendants of Murano's founders, refugees from Altino, and later from Oderzo, who fled from the invading Lombard hordes, as a way of paying homage to the land where their ancestors found shelter.

When it leaves the last landing-stage on "red" Murano, the steamboat slowly ploughs through the liquid plain, studded with sandbanks covered in sun-scorched vegetation and islands with weeping ruins, the last vestiges of ancient communities now extinct, on its way to vibrant Burano. The island of color, an ancient fishing village, has become an artists' colony precisely because it is so colorful. It is a delightful little island, with narrow streets, arched porticoes, miniature canals, washing and fishing nets strung out in the meadows to dry in the sun, and a melodious dialect which, like the language of love, communicates to the heart. The island's most famous citizen could only be a great musician like Baldassare Galuppi who, proudly mindful of his birthplace, took the name of Buranello.

Torcello is right in front of Burano, and in a few minutes it is possible to go ashore to disturb the ancient peace and trample the grassy meadows in which vestiges of an impressive civilization survive. It is hard to imagine that New Altino, where

54-55 Murano, a densely populated island in the lagoon and home of the art of glass-blowing, was founded during the Lombard invasion by a group of refugees from Altino, who called it Amurianum after one of the gates of their city.

54 bottom The Pellestrina littoral, between the ports of Malamocco and Chioggia, with its monumental murazzi (a kind of marble breakwater), demonstrates the Venetians' amazing ability to cope with the threat represented by the sea.

55 top The "pathways" through the lagoon are indicated by the characteristic bricole, sets of wooden poles tied to one another which mark the boundaries of the canals and act as maritime signals.

55 bottom The magnificent external apse of the church of Saints Maria and Donato in Murano, with a portico featuring niches and coupled columns and the bell tower, constitutes one of the best surviving examples of Venetian-Byzantine art, with its blend of Byzantine and Romanesque characteristics and architectural motifs.

56 top left From the bell tower, the complex of religious and lay buildings and the little piazza emerge from the huge stretches of sandbanks that surround this remote, sacred hermitage on Torcello island.

56 bottom left The interior of Santa Maria Assunta on Torcello island features a six columns' iconostasis and four carved plutei. The Madonna and Child are portrayed in the bowl-shaped apse at the end.

56 right The Church of Santa Fosca on Torcello island, with its attractive five-sided portico with raised arches and its austere interior in a Greek cross layout, is typical of sacred Byzantine architecture.

57 The magnificent mosaic on the entrance well of the Basilica of Santa Maria Assunta on Torcello island depicts the Crucifixion and the Last Judgment in accordance with Byzantine iconography.

refugees from the nearby mainland found safety when they fled from the barbarians, could once have had a population of 20,000, as the chronicles report. However, without that impressive community, which had its own bishop and tribune, Torcello would perhaps never have enjoyed the prosperity it needed to sponsor the creation of such marvelous architecture. The delightful little piazza with "Attila's chair" (the seat used by the tribunes when administering the law), the most profaned and photographed sight in Italy, has everything, from the fourteenth-

century Council and Archive buildings, which now house an important museum displaying archaeological relics from the Roman, early Christian, and late Medieval periods, to the religious atmosphere of the little church of Santa Fosca and the monumental complex of the Cathedral of Santa Maria Assunta. However, it is the mosaic of the Universal Judgement that really takes the visitor's breath away. It is easy to understand why a writer like Ernest Hemingway found the peace and quiet he needed to write the best parts of his novel Across The River And Into The Trees in this very hermitage, immersed in nature, peace, spirituality, and history.

From Burano, a convenient motor launch takes us on a short but enjoyable trip across the still waters of the lagoon to Punta Sabbioni, a seaside resort that stretches as far as Cavallino, once part of Venice but now an independent municipality. It boasts famous glasshouses that grow spring vegetables and above all numerous campsites, assiduously frequented by regular customers, mostly Germans, who transform these shores into a German-speaking colony as far as Lido di Jesolo in the summer months. Lido di Jesolo is the loveliest

beach in the Venice area, and is a main attraction because of its wealth of hotels and modern bathing establishments which offer tourists an endless variety of activities, sports, and entertainment, from riding stables to tennis courts, from swimming pools with dizzyingly steep water slides to famous restaurants and discos for lovers of night life. Beyond the Piave estuary lies the more recently developed resort of Eraclea Mare. This magnificent sandy coastline with its highly popular bathing establishments also offers some very attractive spots of historical interest like the ancient town of Caorle, whose unusual cylindrical brick bell-tower with its conical spire provides a look-out point over the vast waters of the Adriatic.

The Venice Lido, with its exclusive bathing establishments, was once the most popular beach with the international jet set. However, its popularity gradually declined in favor of brand-new facilities that met the demands of mass tourism more efficiently. It has now been converted into a huge residential center for Venetians, although the original, attractive Art Nouveau villas and hotels like Grand Hotel Des Bains and the Excelsior Palace Hotel, with its oriental look, still survive. The island rests on the laurels of its magnificent past, and is now satisfied to be back in the limelight once a year during the International Film Festival.

Proceeding to the end of the Lido, a boat can be borded at the picturesque medieval town of Malamocco, named after the ancient Doge's residence of Metamauco, where Charlemagne's son Pippin suffered a crushing defeat when his troops were surrounded by the more agile Venetian vessels. The slaughter was horrific, as testified to by the name of Canal Orfano (Orphan Canal), so called to commemorate the Frankish children orphaned in the battle. A catastrophe then destroyed Metamauco, which sank into the sea and disappeared forever. It was replaced by the delightful Malamocco, which is proud of its Palazzo Pretorio, containing the mayor's offices, the piazza with the Church of St. Maria Assunta, and the characteristic avenue called Merceria which runs through alleys and piazzas to the pretty Ponte di Borgo.

Heading to the south, Pellestrina, a fisherman's island, is a strip of land with numerous arms jutting out into the sea. These murazzi, great walls made of marble blocks cemented with pozzolana, were the pride of the ancient Venetians, built ausu romano, aere veneto (in the Roman style with Venetian cash) to defend the lagoon. Another commemorative tablet dated 1751 proudly states in Latin, "The keepers of the waters

laid colossal blocks of solid marble against the sea so that the sacred estuaries, the site of the city and of freedom, may be preserved in perpetuity."

Tradition has it that after the Chioggia war, four families (the Busetto, Vianello, Zennaro, and Scarpa families) began to rebuild Pellestrina. Everyone on Pellestrina now has one of these surnames, as do the four "quarters" into which the island is divided. These stubborn but hospitable people have their own dialect, which remains distinct from Venetian and outright disdainful of the Chioggia dialect. They are tough people, who came face to face with death during the catastrophic storm of 1966, when the sea threatened to submerge the island together with Venice. Yet, the people of Pellestrina stay. They are attached to their homes and their possessions, like the seaweed that almost clings to their homes, although the island lacks even the most basic, essential amenities and they have to depend on the local markets of the Venice Lido and Chioggia to do their shopping. The last stop on the

island is a small cemetery, too small for all the people so attached to this strip of the lagoon, after which a last promontory narrows towards Caroman, a vernacular corruption of Ca' Romana (Roman House). Sailing between the posts that mark the boundary of the canal and the odd buildings on stilts where fishing equipment is kept, the colors of the water change, and the roofs and spires of Chioggia can be seen in the distance.

Chioggia, the ancient Roman Clodia, is given a majestic appearance by the effects of time and centuriation (the Roman division of land into hundreds). The intersecting Roman roads, the cardo and decumanus, with dozens of little lanes branching off from the bustling Corso del Popolo, transform the layout of the town into a dense herringbone-shaped latticework. This fish metaphor and the inevitable comparison with its aristocratic neighbor suggest that the town is a "little Venice." However, this comparison is not appreciated by its inhabitants, who have no wish to resemble anyone, least of all the Venetians, who in the past granted Chioggia institutions similar to their own but totally devoid of political content, so that its fictitious independence was totally crushed by continual interference from the mayor, who held the central power.

The people of Chioggia have a sanguine nature, a skin dried by long exposure to the sun and the dazzling blue-green water, and talk loudly in a melodious, colorful, sing-song dialect. This habit, acquired over the centuries by a population of fishermen who had to shout from one boat to another and one bank to another, has been retained by the elderly out of inertia and inherited by their descendents. The quarrelsome but good-hearted nature of the people of Chioggia was well understood by a young Venetian who obtained his first job as Assistant Registrar of the Criminal Court, Carlo Goldoni, destined to become a famous playwright. There's no lack of fish and fishing in Chioggia. The very air is impregnated with them, and the rich vocabulary of the Chioggia dialect has numerous words for them. Perhaps attracted by the fish, at the

60 top This wide-angle aerial view clearly shows the unusual structure of Chioggia, deriving from its remote Roman origins, which makes it look oddly like a fishbone.

60 bottom Large, calm reaches of sandbanks covered with sparse vegetation make patterns on the blue waters

of the lagoon, and provide the ideal habitat for seagulls.

61 Canal Vena is one of the most characteristic spots in Chioggia, with its numerous fishing boats, nets hanging out on the bricole, fruit and vegetable stalls, and perpendicular lanes, always buzzing with life.

quay near Ponte di Vigo a curious lion that bears no resemblance to the emblem of Saint Mark, but looks for all the world like a cat, welcomes visitors. "The Chioggia moggy" looks slyly at us, waiting there indifferent to criticism and unmoved by insult, gazing at the sky as if trying to divert the marùbio (tempest), the terror of sailors, portrayed in thousands of colorful, naïve votive offerings displayed for popular veneration in the Church of San Domenico. Thronging the crowded streets, cafés, and inns of Canal Vena, lined with fishing boats, nets, and trammels, baskets firmly imprison struggling crabs which, according to the local dialect, develop from strussi (used as fish bait) to spiantani and then shed their skins to become the delectable moléche. Old men hunched stiffly in the taverns amuse themselves by telling repetitive tales of long-ago feats at sea, while the fumes and fog from their meerschaum pipes shroud them in sadness and resignation. Their stories of hardship and poverty are hard to understand nowadays, in our comfortable, wealthy society, but their bitterness is soon dispelled over a glass of wine. There, amid the confused hum of conversations, the "sweet sound of life" can be heard placidly flowing by.

Eleonora Duse's grandfather Luigi, the last representative of the noble dynasty of Commedia dell'Arte, lived in one of the lanes running perpendicular to Canal Vena. He acted with an amateur dramatic society, then joined a repertory company and spawned a whole family of actors. Applauded on stage and even mentioned by George Sand in Histoire De Ma Vie, he certainly never expected to be remembered as the august ancestor of one of the greatest actresses of the twentieh century. He could have been born nowhere else but in this theatrical city, where Carlo Goldoni looked out of his window onto Corso del Popolo every day and smiled as he watched the hard-working people of Chioggia with their drawling dialect, who were forced to invent imaginative nicknames for themselves (or "aliases," as they are called locally) because so many of them have the same surnames.

Whatever happened to the colorful bragozzi, the characteristic fishing boats? A fleet is now anchored in Canal Lombardo which runs parallel to the main street, its forest of masts bristling with the most sophisticated fishing and navigation technologies. The poor old bragozzo has become merely a souvenir, a model sold to tourists or a cult object for rich collectors who like to stand out from the crowd and from real fishermen. They sail proudly over the waters of the port like ghosts, flying gaudy

62 top and top center
The Delta area holds some surprises in store for nature lovers. In addition to the sedentary and migratory wild life, there are also fish-farms, which exploit large stretches of briny water to breed mollusks.

62 bottom center Fishing is one of the major sources of income in the Delta area. This photo shows a typical fisherman's cottage.

flags and colorful red and ochre sails bearing the emblems and coats-of-arms of days gone by.

Before leaving Chioggia, it is worth crossing the long bridge with the Island of Union in the middle (an inappropriate name if ever there was one), a long umbilical cord that links Chioggia to Sottomarina, where some equally odd people await. However, it is important to drop the first part of the name of the town upon crossing that bridge because the people of Sottomarina call themselves marinanti and will be very annoyed if they are called anything else.

Leaving behind the bickering of these populations, condemned to be eternally quarrelsome in accordance with literary tradition, one can travel to Polesine, the southernmost tip of Veneto, where the last reaches of the Po flow across the plain to the sea, and the great river "finds peace with all its followers" as Dante put it (Inferno, V 98). The plain lying between the Rivers Adige and Po is composed of vast wetlands formed over geological time by the accumulation of silt deposited by the two great rivers. Although this abundance of water is vital for agricultural purposes, it is also a cause of concern. The administrators of the past decided that these waters should be regulated with embankments and artificial canals to avoid disaster, which is why complex hydrographic schemes have been constructed over the centuries, although these efforts have often been tragically thwarted by devastating floods.

The delta region, constantly shrouded in spirals of fog, is the true queen of the area. The Po Delta is a magical spot, fortunately still partly unspoiled, though menaced by a tourist industry attracted by the idea of the huge profits expected to be generated by a controversial park scheme. This "water province" is also beloved of cinema directors, especially the great Roberto Rossellini, who shot one of the most gripping scenes of partisan warfare in the last episode of Paisà there. Michelangelo Antonioni also celebrated Polesine in The Outcry, a tragic love story which was being filmed in the winter of 1956 when the Po burst its banks and displayed all its terrible brute force, dictating its own terms to the director and forcing him to make cuts in the script. This friendly river, yet at times so disquieting and hostile, has left its mark on the people of Polesine. However much they may suffer, they can rarely tear themselves away from this wildly beautiful spot. The best way of getting to know the river is by boat, meditating on the skilled gestures of the

62 bottom The low herbaceous vegetation, characterized by marsh samphire, sea-lavender, and reeds, is typical of these marshy areas of the Po Delta close to the sea.

62-63 A lovely sunset in the Po Delta. The sun sends out its last gleams of fire before drowning in the water, revealing the outlines of the isolated huts used to store fishing gear.

elderly boatmen, the silence of the area and the incredible charm bestowed on it by the flora and fauna, the latter often being the only constant companion in these remote districts. Towns and cities are scattered all around, such as Rovigo, the agricultural capital of Polesine, which also has an important cultural heritage as witnessed by the Accademia dei Concordi, Lendinara, and finally Adria. It's hard to imagine when visiting this small town that long ago, under Greek occupation, it was so important as to be considered the main trading center in the Po Valley. Then the Etruscans arrived, followed by the Romans, who ennobled it with their presence, and it became such an important town that its name was given to the Adriatic Sea, now some 12 miles away from Adria because of the continual advance of the delta.

These lands are imbued with magic. While watching one of their fiery sunsets it is easy to understand why the myth of Phaeton was set here. Phaeton stole the chariot of the sun, but in his youthful inexperience he was unable to control the reins of the prancing horses, and burned the Earth and the Sky. The solemn Zeus intervened, and hurled the imprudent charioteer into the River Po. His sisters, the Heliades, mourned his death, and moved the gods so much that they turned them into poplars out of compassion. Those same trees still offer generous shade to the incurable romantics who walk these streets, day-dreaming of the ancient fables and musing on the profound significance of the old adage "The Po is born where the scent of the sea is in the air." Recalling the myth and the proverb, we finally realize that the palpable sweetness of these lovely wild spots has all the passion of an ancient lament behind it.

PADUA AND THE BRENTA RIVIERA, TREVISO AND THE "JOYFUL REGION"

64 top This delightful country residence, built by Andrea Palladio for the nobleman Leonardo Emo at Fanzolo, in the Treviso region, is a classic mansion with porticoed canopy roofs at the sides.

64-65 Immersed in lush vegetation, Villa Foscari, traditionally known as "La Malcontenta," is one of the gems built by Palladio on the banks of the River Brenta.

65 top Villa Nani Mocenigo, widely believed to have been designed by Vincenzo Scamozzi, stands on the banks of the Canalbianco at Canda, in the province of Rovigo.

Leaving Fusina behind us after taking our leave of Venice, we follow the road that leads, as in the past, towards the "delights of the River Brenta." Of course, we can no longer enjoy the pleasure of embarking on the burchiello, *a little river boat decorated with mirrors, carvings, and paintings, which used to be towed across the lagoon to the mainland by a tug and then pulled by horses led along the towpath. In* Arcadia in Brenta ovvero la melanconia sbandita (Arcadia in Brenta, Or Melancholy Banished), *Giovanni Sagredi describes the craft as "a mobile room, a floating apartment."*

Carlo Goldoni gives a similar description, set at a time when the Venetians of the ancient Republic longed for summer and autumn holidays, and those who could afford them swarmed merrily to spend their days of leisure amid the amusements that the magnificent villas built along the "placid river" reserved for the idle rich. But what delights were in store for the "young gentlemen," the last squanderers of what was often a meager inheritance, already laid waste by generations of spendthrifts? Father Goldoni acts as our guide, explaining the motivation behind all these desires - luxury, opulence, and the vices of gambling and love - which while on vacation could be enjoyed with greater freedom than in the strictly supervised drawing rooms of Venetian villas, where tyrannical fathers, virtuous mothers, and a swarm of servants always willing to act the spy meant that privacy was non-existent.

Although this was the reigning way of life as the libertine period of the early eighteenth century drew to a close, life in the sixteenth century must have been very different, as we are reminded by the magnificent Villa Foscari, known as La Malcontenta (Villa of Discontent). A pretty young woman, one Elisabetta Dolfin, who had proved rather too fond of worldly pleasures in licentious Venice, had been severely punished for her lascivious behavior by being shut away in that gilded cage, designed by Andrea Palladio for brothers Nicolò and Luigi Foscari. Set amid a profusion of greenery, where the fronds of the weeping willows that bow gently down to the waters of a loop of a navigable canal conceal just enough of the magnificent architecture to frame it, the villa can only be compared with the garden of Eden. However, as a Venetian proverb has it, "being all alone is no fun, not even in paradise." This romantic story has become legendary, and a portrait of a woman by Giambattista Zelotti in one of the frescoed rooms of the villa is widely believed to depict Elisabetta. All that luxury was not enough to dispel the cravings of a young woman addicted to pleasure. What a waste, yet one can't help feeling envious; those ancient Venetians certainly lived well.

Another princely mansion, Villa Widmann Rezzonico Foscari, stands just outside Mira. Here, the architecture is more modest and the architect is unknown. The original nucleus dating from 1719, perhaps designed by Tirali, has been rebuilt on numerous occasions. The villa is impressive, with its great French rococo ballroom decorated with frescoes framed by stucco work, and the magnificent paintings remind the visitor that the Widmanns, noble Carinthian merchants, were related to the

Rezzonico family, one of whose members, the future Pope Clement XIII, spent happy days in the villa as a cardinal, unaware that one day he would be weighed down with the cares of the Papacy.

A few miles beyond Dolo, just outside Stra, stands the most attractive and magnificent villa on the Brenta Riviera: Villa Pisani, known as La Nazionale. At the height of the decadence of Venice, in 1735, Alvise Pisani had been elected Doge, and the mansion, commissioned from Gerolamo Frigimelica and continued after the architect's death by Francesco Maria Preti, was almost finished. The building is truly impressive; the interior consists of 114 rooms frescoed by the best artists of the period, including Ricci, Zais, and Zuccarelli, while the Apotheosis of the Pisani Family in the central hall was painted by the great Giambattista

Tiepolo. Famous guests who have stayed at the villa include Napoleon, Maria Luigia of Parma, Maximilian of Hapsburg, Tsar Alexander I, Vittorio Emanuele II of Savoy and, in 1934, Hitler and Mussolini.

Huge grounds with stables and fishponds and the "frescoed house" on the hill, welcome visitors, but the great attraction of the villa is its maze, a mysterious route running between box hedges, a source of amusement designed by a whimsical gardener for the enjoyment of ladies and gentlemen during the era of beauty spots, powder, and crinolines. It has now been restored to its original splendor, but when D'Annunzio described it in Fuoco, it had run wild, and the rusty, squeaking gate led to a tangled excess of vegetation. However, in that neglected state it was perhaps better able to liberate the hero's sensual capacity, his sensitivity towards the

66 top One of the 114 rooms furnished with exquisite eighteenth-century pieces which form the gigantic Villa Pisani complex in Stra is named after Bacchus.

66 bottom The Pisani family, which had achieved an important position among the Venetian nobility, commissioned Tiepolo to paint the Apotheosis of the family on the ballroom ceiling.

66-67 With its huge grounds, stables, and the famous maze, immortalized in D'Annunzio's novel Fuoco, the majestic Villa Pisani, known as "La Nazionale," at Stra on the Brenta Riviera, is a mansion worthy of a Doge.

spirits of nature, and his eventual communion
with forest life. Real mazes and the mazes of the
soul: a magical coincidence. The father of Italian
psychoanalysis, Cesare Musatti, was born just a
stone's throw away from this enchanting,
romantic spot, and on the very same day,
September 21, 1897, Sigmund Freud passed by
on his way to Venice. On the same day he
expounded on his new theory in a letter to
Fliess, which is why Musatti jokingly called
psychoanalysis "my twin sister." Be that as it
may, there are really too many coincidences,
and the real or imaginary labyrinth becomes
ever more intricate!

   Leaving the magic of the Brenta Riviera
behind, Padua, City of the Saint, lies ready to
welcome. Ancient mythology has been invoked
to account for the foundation of Padua, which
antedates Rome, and the choice fell on the
Trojan Antenor, presumably a character of little
virtue, because in accordance with a late post-
Homeric interpretation, Dante gave his name to
one of the circles in the lower inferno to which
traitors to their country were assigned
(Inferno, XXXII, 88). Padua was later given a
new aura of respectability as the City of the
Saint, the saint in question being the best loved
in the world, Saint Anthony of Lisbon, who was
so impressed by the simplicity and humility of
the first Franciscan monks that he serenely
embarked on the career of preacher, and ended
his days in this remote spot before passing on to
celestial beatitude in heaven. Padua, a
university town with an illustrious academic
history, is a city of "great scholars" according
to tradition, but also fond of a joke. The
university is called the "Bo" (the ox) by the
locals, because it stands on the site of an ancient
inn that bore the sign of an ox. The university
was founded in 1222, and Galileo Galilei gave
lectures freely there before being lured away by
the more attractive financial offer made by
Grand Duke Cosimo II. Unfortunately, there

70 top *The Law Courts were once housed in Palazzo della Ragione, in this huge hall with its magnificent roof shaped like the hull of a ship.*

were some very unpleasant surprises in store for him when it came to freedom of thought.

Albertino Mussato, Alvise Cornaro, and Angelo Beolco, better known as Ruzante, are some of the most famous graduates of the university, that great melting pot of Paduan culture. In more recent times, playwright Carlo Goldoni obtained a law degree from the university, although he preferred theatrical to legal oratory. Another student, Giacomo Casanova, while attending law school there, had not yet decided between an ecclesiastical career and the libertine vocation to which he eventually devoted body and soul with truly laudable dedication.

Padua is a city of art, offering a wealth of paintings and architecture, from the Roman Patavium, an opulent and densely populated city of the Roman Empire, the remains of which are to be found everywhere, to the medieval Palazzo della Ragione and the beloved Basilica of the Saint, built to house the precious remains of Saint Anthony. Later graced by Giotto's prestigious frescoes in the chapel dedicated by Enrico Scrovegni to the memory of his father (who was included among the usurers in

70-71 The walls of the Great Hall of Padua's Palazzo della Ragione are covered with fresco cycles featuring a mixture of sacred and profane themes, including the astrological series inspired by the writings of famous doctor and astrologer Pietro d'Abano.

71 top The Romanesque-Gothic Eremitani Church, which was seriously damaged by bombing in 1944, was rebuilt to restore at least fragments of the magnificent frescoes painted by Mantegna.

71 bottom The huge fruit and vegetable market has always been held in Piazza delle Erbe and under the porticoes of Palazzo della Ragione.

72 top The interior of St. Anthony's Basilica, divided into a nave and two aisles, has a Latin cross layout. Galleries run along the walls, and the interior space is dominated by the huge vaults of the domes.

72 bottom Pilgrims from all over the world flock to St. Anthony's Basilica to pay homage to St. Anthony of Lisbon, who rests in peace for all eternity in Padua.

Dante's **Inferno**) in 1305, Padua became a center of the arts in the fourteenth century. However, it was Tuscan artist Giusto de' Menabuoi and above all Donatello who brought to life the miracles of Saint Anthony in the reliefs on the high altar of the Basilica. Donatello also sculpted the equestrian statue of Erasmo da Narni, known as Gattamelata, in homage to a military leader who had valiantly served the Republic of Venice, which still ruled Padua. Andrea Mantegna did some of his best work in the Eremitani Church, but much of it was destroyed in a devastating bombing raid in 1944. However, the Ovetari Chapel still contains at least one sample of his work.

The city offers nature lovers the oldest Botanical Garden in the world. It was founded in 1545 by resolution of the Senate of the Veneto Republic to grow medicinal plants, and exotic

72-73 St. Anthony's Basilica is an architectural complex featuring an astonishing blend of Romanesque and Gothic elements and even Islamic style, as in the bell towers, which strongly resemble minarets.

73 The high altar of the Presbytery of St. Anthony's Basilica, designed by Donatello, was totally rebuilt in the late nineteenth century. The restructuring work was controversial, but at least the bronzes by Donatello and his school were preserved.

plants from various parts of the world were added over the centuries, until it became a center of cultivation and research of enviable international prestige.

Padua is best appreciated on foot, strolling past the noisy stalls of the markets in Piazza delle Erbe, sizing up Piazza dei Signori from the porticoes, or visiting one of the biggest piazzas in Italy, Prato della Valle (Valley Meadow), which is surrounded by an elliptical canal and sits on the site where the Roman amphitheater

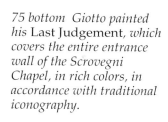

75 bottom Giotto painted his Last Judgement, which covers the entire entrance wall of the Scrovegni Chapel, in rich colors, in accordance with traditional iconography.

74-75 and 75 top The simple, aisle-less structure of the Scrovegni Chapel in Padua is entirely covered by Giotto's masterpiece depicting stories of Mary and Christ, divided into three strips and 38 panels.

74 bottom left Giotto's intense vision of the Flight to Egypt is set in a landscape dominated by a pyramid-shaped spur of rock, against which the protagonists stand out.

74 bottom right On this panel in the Chapel, Giotto depicts the episode in which an angel announces the future birth of the Virgin Mary to her father, Joachim, in a dream.

once stood. However, the true atmosphere of the city can be breathed in the famous "doorless" Café Pedrocchi, which was built in the style of a Neoclassical temple. There, in the cold silence of the marble interior, possibly in contrast with the jesting young voice of a new graduate giving his first mock public speech in front of the café in accordance with custom, the visitor begins to enter into the spirit of this singular city, whose emblem is oddness and gaiety. With his usual elegance and erudition Toni Cibotto, the famous author, told me the popular saying which gives an illuminating perception of the character of the city: "Padua, the city that has a café with no doors, a meadow with no grass, and a saint with no name."

Because of the traffic and pollution that besiege all big cities, and Padua in particular, those fine, clear days that reveal the miracle of the nearby Euganean Hills are becoming increasingly rare. The durable trachyte that

paves many cities used to be quarried in these hills, and their volcanic origin is demonstrated by the numerous hot springs from which emerge rivers of miracle-working mud, essential for curing arthritis and rheumatism, that has made the fortune of well-known local spas like Abano, Montegrotto, and Battaglia Terme. With their conical and rounded shapes, covered with copses, locust trees, and hazel groves, the Euganean hills, named after a population that lived in the area in ancient times, have existed since time immemorial, a reassuring, cheering sight. It must be these delightful features which have made them the home of poets, such as the tired old Petrarch, who preferred to spend the last years of his old age among the olive groves

76 top In a stretch of countryside in the Treviso Marches, the medieval tower of Roganzuolo Castle keeps watch over the plain. The castles, fortresses, and walled towns of Veneto, monuments of fear that are still perfectly preserved, constitute one of the many attractions of this region.

76 bottom This lovely view of the Alpago Pre-Alps, a high wall between the Piave and Cellina rivers features a profusion of greenery and nature. The Veneto Pre-Alpine area features mountains of altitudes ranging between 2300 and 7300 feet.

76-77 Silence reigns supreme in the endless vineyards near Combai, known for producing an excellent, light, sparkling Prosecco. Veneto offers many oases of nature and peace, together with the artificial paradises of the palate along its wine and food routes.

78-79 *Because of its
strategic position,
Montagnana was given
stout medieval walls, which
have withstood the ravages
of time. They still protect
the town today for a length
of more than a mile, giving
it an austere look.*

and vineyards of the picturesque, quiet town of Arquà, which now bears his revered name. In Ugo Foscolo's **Jacopo Ortis**, the bad mood of the hero, "angry with the deities of the fatherland" and with Napoleon for having ceded Venice to Austria, is dispelled by the fresh air of these hills, and at least for a little while he is reconciled to the world by his tender love for the beautiful Teresa. However, he also expresses his indignation at the appalling neglect of Petrarch's house, reduced to a heap of ruins overrun by nettles and weeds. Fortunately, his poetic plea was heard, recorded for posterity, and granted.

Tranquility of soul and mind is also to be found in the Benedictine monastery of Praglia, where the monks still live in a timeless age, tending medicinal plants or restoring precious

79 top right Castelfranco, the birthplace of Giorgione, is distinguished from the other walled towns of Veneto by its castle, whose construction was ordered by Treviso. This photo shows St. Mark's lion and the clock on the Civic Tower.

79 bottom The unusual Villa Giustinian (now known as Villa Ciani-Bassetti) at Roncade was built towards the end of the fifteenth century in the form of a medieval castle.

manuscripts. However, this peace visibly clashes with the numerous remains of turreted and walled cities like Monselice Castle, residence of the fierce Ezzelino da Romano, Este Castle, and especially the endless medieval brick walls which have defended Montagnana for centuries and constitute one of the best examples of ancient fortifications in Europe. War and peace, tranquil abbeys and lonely hermitages or the distant sound of war trumpets; all the charm and incredible appeal of these lovely spots is

80-81 This picturesque view of the porticoes overlooking Canale dei Buranelli shows one of the loveliest spots in Treviso.

80 bottom The sixteenth-century walls and monumental city gates give Treviso the severe look of an ancient medieval town.

81 Treviso's amazing labyrinth of canals, and the confluence of the River Botteniga (called the Cagnano in ancient times) with the crystal-clear waters of the River Sile, have justly earned it the nickname of "city of water."

summed up in this obvious contradiction.

When Petrarch wrote of "clear, fresh, sweet waters," he was inspired by the crystal-clear River Sorga near Valchiusa, but the same poetic impression is received when standing on Dante's Bridge at Treviso and looking down, as the stone tablet says, at the spot "where Sile and Cagnan come together" (Paradiso, IX, 49). Although the River Cagnan is now called the Botteniga, Treviso still remains the "city of water," with its numerous canals and karstic springs. It's a medieval city, a painted town, where the façades of the houses display the faded remnants of gaudy ancient tapestries, with coats of arms and ornaments to demonstrate

*82 The Chapter-house of
the Dominicans in the
former Monastery of St.
Nicolò in Treviso is
decorated with frescoes by
Tomaso da Modena,
famous because they
constitute the first
documented evidence of the
use of spectacles.*

their kinship to noble families that are now wholly extinct. Piazza dei Signori and Palazzo dei Trecento recall medieval splendors that have fallen into oblivion for centuries. These roads were once traveled by dashing squires and seraphic Dominican monks, like those humorously portrayed by the great illustrator Tomaso da Modena in the chapter-house of San Nicolò, absorbed in their studies, with eyes so weakened by long and sometimes tedious reading that they required the aid of the first spectacles recorded in history.

Treviso emerges from the waters like an island, as does the delightful fish market in its fairytale setting. Not far away, the vanes of derelict watermills keep turning impassively, while the waters flow quietly all around. These placid waters are disturbed only by a trout suddenly darting to the surface, or the quacking of a mallard as it crossly follows an over-impertinent companion, while from the height of its mute, regal inscrutability a swan,

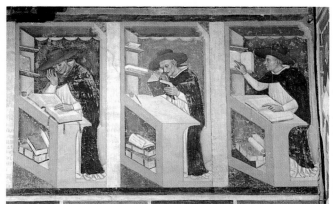

82-83 The busy Piazza dei Signori, with its welcoming porticoes and elegant shops and cafés, is the showplace of Treviso and a popular meeting place with its inhabitants.

83 40 panels painted by Tomaso da Modena depict the most famous personalities of the Dominican order, absorbed in reading in their lonely cells.

84 top Via XX Settembre, with its wide porticoes flanked by ancient palazzi, is the main road running through Conegliano.

84 top Via XX Settembre, with its wide porticoes flanked by ancient palazzi, *is the main road running through Conegliano.*

with sinuously elegant movements, observes the quiet, eternal flow of the river. Yet modernity also puts in an appearance here, in the scintillating windows of the luxurious shops under the welcoming porticoes of the main street called Calmaggiore. The girls strolling down the street are proverbially beautiful, the very same girls who inspired film director Pietro Germi to expose the subtle erotic subterfuges and hypocrisy of seemingly respectable married folk in Signore e Signori.

Treviso is also the capital of what used to be known as the "Joyful Region," and it certainly deserves that epithet, if only for the geographical beauty of its districts and the fertile land on which towns like Conegliano are built, surrounded by vineyards famed for their white prosecco. Castelvecchio (the old castle), built in the tenth century and included under the rule of Verona and Venice, stands in the walled town of that medieval fortress, which has existed for centuries, and still retains traces of its noble past. Conegliano was the birthplace of Cima, who ennobled the town with his magical brush. Other ancient towns also produced some great painters, like Castelfranco Veneto, the birthplace of Giorgione, where more city walls and another defensive castle can be seen. However, it is at Asolo, the home of Caterina Cornaro, Queen of Cyprus, where we really become immersed in history. Its severe fortress dominates the area, offering a delightful view over the hills and lush vegetation from which Asolo emerges supreme. It is imbued with an incredible charm, which is why it was chosen as their home by many famous personalities such as Bembo, Giorgione, Eleonora Duse, and Robert Browning. Even the unusually tame-looking lion lying on the great fountain seems

84 bottom The Strada del Vino Bianco (White Wine Road), which leads from Conegliano to Valdobbiadene, offers some lovely, surprising, hilly landscapes, as shown in this view, looking towards the small town of Costa.

84-85 Conegliano, originally a walled town, still retains some of its Medieval charm, especially in the characteristic "bell tower," which now houses the Civic Castle Museum.

85 bottom The fortress, with the encircling walls descending towards the castle, offers a severe image of placid Asolo, nestling in a landscape that exudes peace and quiet. The humanistic court of noblemen and artists with which Caterina Cornaro, Queen of Cyprus, surrounded herself restored the peace she needed after the dramatic family events she had experienced, and changed the face of this delightful town for all time.

86 top The real genius of Palladio lay in the skill with which he blended his architectural creations, consisting of porticoes, nyphaeum, fishponds, dovecotes, and gardens, with the magnificent geographical position of Maser, molded by nature.

86 center Veronese lavished all his genius on the cross-vaults of Villa Barbaro, inventing a rustic concert with musicians, singers, pages, and curious little girls peeping out from behind imitation doors.

86 bottom The large, well-lit rooms of Villa Barbaro display the pictorial genius of Paolo Veronese, who was commissioned to paint the frescoes, while Alessandro Vittoria made the stucco mouldings and the numerous sculptures.

87 Villa Barbaro, in Maser, was commissioned from Palladio in 1560 by Daniele Barbaro, Patriarch of Aquileia, and his brother Marcantonio, Ambassador of the Venetian Republic.

88-89 This field of sunflowers in the Treviso region is a blaze of color.

to feel very much at home here, and has nothing of the arrogant, aggressive pose typical of its counterparts throughout the dominions of Veneto, which are always portrayed standing, looking proudly ahead. We certainly can't fault the artist's choice. Everything here is conducive to the serenity of the soul and gaiety of spirit.

If we also want to find art, we need only walk a little way to visit Villa Barbaro at Maser, where Andrea Palladio, Paolo Veronese, and Alessandro Vittoria created a true miracle. Daniele, Patriarch of Aquileia, and his brother Marcantonio Barbaro, Ambassador of the Republic of Venice, were learned humanists and erudite scholars, and their villa speaks for itself. It was designed by Palladio in accordance with the rules of harmonic proportions he himself laid down: "A city should be none other than a great house, and conversely, a house should be a small city." The astute Barbaro family were very far-sighted; only art could make them immortal, and they are all still there to welcome us. Marcantonio's beloved wife Giustiniana Giustiniani, portrayed accompanied by a nurse, leans over the balcony, while all round, nature plays the daintiest of minuets in and out of the imitation pergolas, and the painted landscapes seem to break through the walls. In other portraits, a page spies on visitors from behind a door, and a curious, smiling little girl who has come to hide in this very room suddenly realizes she has been discovered, almost seeming to protest that the intrusion has disturbed her game. Leaving her there in peace, silently playing her childish games, she has been eternally condemned to this happy fate by the hand of an unusual and very whimsical artist.

90 top left   Vicenza, city of the arts, offers numerous opportunities and places of rare beauty in which everyone can refine and stimulate their own talents in an endless variety of styles and inspired combinations.

90 top right   This photo shows a detail of the façade of the Church of San Vincenzo in Vicenza's Piazza dei Signori, with its unmistakable bell tower.

VICENZA, VERONA, AND LAKE GARDA

Vicenza and Andrea Palladio are inseparable. Palladio, the architect from Padua, had the pulsating heart of an entire city as the testing ground for his genius, but he also had the luck to encounter a rich caste of ambitious Vicenza men who were constantly competing with Venice and happy to loosen their purse-strings if it meant making a good impression. Vicenza already had its Gothic Ca' d'oro, but without the Grand Canal to reflect it, it could hardly compete with the buildings of Venice. Vicenza also boasted the unique, picturesque Casa Pigafetta, in which Gothic, Spanish, and early Renaissance architecture are extravagantly combined. However, as the family motto of Antonio Pigafetta, the navigator who accompanied Magellan's voyage round the world, puts it, "There's no rose without a thorn," and for the people of Vicenza, envy was a real thorn in the flesh. If Vicenza is still counted among the great cities of art today, it is largely due to those ancient philanthropists and to Andrea Palladio. Yet Palladio's relationship with the city was uneasy to begin with, and clearly full of suspicion. In fact, although the architect had brilliantly resolved the problem of restoring the Gothic palazzo, with its magnificent marble facing and serliana windows, in an outstanding design presented to the High Council in 1546, the work was postponed because the city's administrators decided to submit the plan to the judgment of the entire community. The arch was meanwhile built of wood and abandoned for nearly two years, until the resolution was finally passed by 99 votes to 17 on April 11, 1549.

Palladio made his name with the monumental Basilica in Piazza dei Signori, his first public building, but his fame and fortune came thanks to his benefactor, Giangiorgio Trissino. Andrea, son of miller Pietro della Gondola and his wife, nicknamed "lame Marta," would never have achieved much success if it hadn't been for

91 top Palazzo della Ragione, universally known by the name of "Basilica," was the first public building to be designed in Vicenza by Palladio, who brilliantly solved the problem by enclosing the existing Gothic structure in elegant classical loggias.

91 bottom This photo shows the monumental stage of the Olympic Theater, the oldest surviving indoor theater, which was built by Palladio for the Academy of the same name. It was inaugurated on March 3, 1585 with a performance of Sophocles' Oedipus Rex.

92-93 Vicenza is situated in a delightful position at the foot of the Berici Mountains, embellished by the confluence of the Retrone and Bacchiglione rivers which surround the city.

his encounter with that famous man of letters, who was a veritable talent scout. Andrea, "son of Pietro of Padua," took the name of Palladio, in accordance with the rhetoric of the humanistic culture and custom of the day, in gratitude to the man who had introduced him to the beauties of classical art in Rome. Palladio amply repaid his debt of gratitude not only to his illustrious discoverer, but to all his less prominent fellow citizens.

Palladio and the rational forms of his buildings are ever-present in Vicenza, from the Loggia del Capitanato to Palazzo Chiericati, which now houses the Civic Museum, from Palazzo Marcantonio Thiene to his masterpiece, the Olimpico Theater, which was his last great work. The theater is so magical that although it was built in haste like many Renaissance theaters and perhaps not destined to survive for

92 bottom and 93 Some wonderful views can be seen from the ancient bridges over the River Bacchiglione, such as the impressive verdigris-covered roof of the Basilica, which towers over the surrounding buildings.

94-95 The Sanctuary of Mount Berico, on a shady green hillside overlooking Vicenza, offers a magnificent view of the city.

long after the production of Sophocles' Oedipus Rex during the 1585 carnival, it still stands today as an artistic testament, the glorious beauty of its Vitruvian forms still intact. The only arbitrary license that has been taken with it is represented by the trompe l'oeuil perspectives of the permanent wooden sets built by Vincenzo Scamozzi, who took over the supervision of the work after Palladio's death.

But it was in villas like the famous Villa Capra, known all over the world as La Rotonda that Palladio expressed the best of his ability.

Here, the architect fell in love with the landscape, and saw the need for harmony between ancient forms and nature, as he wrote in his Quattro Libri dell'Architettura. He was certainly aided by the site, a delightful spot on the top of a small hill from which an outstanding view can be seen. The hills all round, covered with lush vineyards, appear to the artist's eye like a great stage offering views on every side. This is why the villa has four temple-style elevations with wide steps to demonstrate the sense of holiness that emanates from that landscape, to which no face can be shown other than the unique, palpitating features of the god of nature who lives there. Rational classical forms are married with the delights of the surrounding environment in a true natural theater, which meant designing buildings in accordance with the rules of harmony laid down by the ancients. Apollo and Dionysus represent reason and irrationality, as in love, where the imprudent irresponsibility of the lover contrasts with the subtle strategy of the seducer, who weaves his fine web with an ever tighter net. That's why Joseph Losey located his Don Giovanni in this setting, which is both natural and artificial at the same time. The same face appears on all sides and everything revolves around it, as in Mozart's opera. It makes no difference whether Don Giovanni is present or absent: everyone talks about him and his amazing prowess as an shameless rake.

The charm that emanates from the peaceful surrounding landscape is equally irresistible. The greenery of the Berici mountains seems to have been specifically designed to act as a backdrop to Arcadia, and the two Tiepolos, father and son, did some of their best work in the nearby Villa Valmarana. Giambattista Tiepolo painted his epic and chivalrous cycle, ranging from The Iliad to Orlando Furioso, from The Aeneid to Jerusalem Delivered, apparently more interested in "women, courtesies, and loves" than in "knights, arms, and audacious feats." In the guest quarters, Giandomenico Tiepolo, free of his father's oppressive influence, depicted his beloved carnival costumes, mountebanks, Commedia dell'Arte characters, and the marvels of the cosmorama or the magic lantern of the "New World." With deft brushstrokes he sometimes portrayed the Venetians under the subtle spell of carnival time, refreshing their spirits by taking a holiday among country people gathered around a fragrant table, or enjoying a well-deserved siesta, and sometimes invented a fantastic Orient, based on the writings of Marco Polo and the fairytale atmospheres of Carlo Gozzi.

96 Villa Valmarana ai Nani, situated in an enviable position on the road leading to Mount Berico, is famous for the cycle of frescoes painted by Giambattista Tiepolo soon after his return from Würzburg.

97 top left Villa Capra, known as "La Rotonda," is the most famous building designed by Andrea Palladio. The sun can be enjoyed all day long at the top of this delightful knoll, where the four identical pronaos façades have a precise astronomical orientation.

97 center left Villa Chiericati-Lambert at Longa di Schiavon in the province of Vicenza, which was built in 1560 but later given a new, Neoclassical façade, contains frescoes painted by a disciple of Paolo Veronese.

97 bottom left This fresco in Villa Valmarana ai Nani, painted by Giambattista Tiepolo, portrays Aeneas presenting Cupid to Dido in the guise of his son Ascanius.

97 top right Villa Valmarana ai Nani, was built by Antonio Muttoni in 1669.

98 top The buildings in Piazza dei Signori, Verona, where Ugo Zannoni's famous monument to Dante of 1865 stands, feature a wide variety of styles which blend perfectly with one another.

The province of Vicenza has bitter memories of World War I, which are hard to eradicate from a population that suffered terribly under occupation. However, the noisy reunions of the veterans and new recruits to the Alpine troops seem to have repressed the pain and suffering experienced during the long period of trench warfare, especially after the rout at Caporetto, when the defense of the River Piave and Monte Grappa was entrusted to 18-year-old recruits. It's enough to hear a choir singing "We'll Shake Hands On Bassano Bridge" over a glass of grappa, the democratic queen that does not disdain the humblest table and "burns up your troubles" according to the country adage, to witness the triumph of good humor and conviviality.

Sitting around a massive table in the oldest grappa tavern in Italy, founded in 1779, before an interminable row of copper vats on the Alpine Troops Bridge at Bassano del Grappa and watching the tumultuous waters of the River Brenta flowing beneath the window, we understand that although war, devastation, bombing, and floods have done their worst, they could not prevail against the stubborn will of these people. They have learned, at a price, how to survive beyond the time allowed by fate, just like that wooden bridge designed by Palladio with its magical row of wooden pillars, which has often been destroyed, but always been rebuilt "just as it used to be."

Marostica, not far from Bassano, was once ruled by the Della Scala family, and its two castles, the upper castle clinging to the hillside and the lower castle overlooking the piazza named after it, suggest that the medieval town was forced by bellicose neighbors to build impregnable defensive ramparts. However, disputes, especially over affairs of the heart, were sometimes easily solved without bloodshed, perhaps over a chessboard, in accordance with a tradition recently rediscovered among the dusty yellowed parchments in the castle archives. The ancient document contains an order originally issued by Cangrande della Scala, and later confirmed by the Doge of Venice, and strictly prohibited duels between noblemen and knights "in memory of the unhappy lovers Lady Juliet Capulet and Lord Romeo Montague," increased the penalties for disobedience, and ordered that the challenge "should be fought out over a noble game of chess."

98 center The Loggia del Consiglio in Piazza dei Signori is a masterpiece of the Verona Renaissance period which, according to tradition, was built by Dominican monk Fra' Giocondo towards the end of the fifteenth century to house the City Council.

98 bottom The Scala Arches, a detail of which is shown here, are the monumental tombs of the lords of Verona, and considered a masterpiece of Gothic funerary art.

98-99 In Roman times, the Forum stood in Verona's Piazza delle Erbe. Now, as shown in this aerial photo, it is the site of a busy market selling fruit, vegetables, flowers, and plants.

99 bottom The crenellated Scala bridge over the River Adige, with its three red brick arches, which was seriously damaged during the Second World War and perfectly rebuilt, gives access to the Castelvecchio defensive complex.

Cangrande, a historical character, and the tragic story of the two lovers, the "poor sacrifices of enmity," which is such a romantic legend that it has almost gained factual status, are typical of Verona, a city where history and fantasy are intermingled more than anywhere else. This *colonia augusta* contains some well-preserved Roman ruins, including a theater used for modern performances and an arena where grand operas are staged today, with "celestial Aida" and the triumphal marches of Radames taking the place of combat between men and wild beasts and mock naval battles. Arias instead of gladiators: magical Verona could not ask for more.

Verona also offers the spectacular Castelvecchio and the River Adige which flows placidly under the arches of the crenellated Scaligero bridge, from which visitors can look down onto the water as they stroll, imagining

the city's medieval past and daydreaming of ladies, knights, and courtly love. In the Church of Santa Anastasia, Pisanello's fine brushstrokes depict holy warriors with their steeds caparisoned in a more festive than warlike way, liberating towns from terrible fire-breathing dragons, and impassive princesses with angelic profiles who seem to be more concerned about keeping their elaborate hairstyles in place than about the fate of the curly-haired, effeminate blond knight who could not look less like Saint George.

100 top left This photo shows one of the odd "hunchbacks" of Sant'Anastasia which support the holy water stoups. According to tradition, they are effigies of millers from the Adige watermills.

100 bottom left St. Zeno's Gate is covered with 48 bronze panels depicting episodes from the life of St. Zeno, allegorical figures, and Biblical stories.

100 top right The Romanesque cloister of St. Zeno is built round a grassy area. It has a large portico with red marble coupled columns supporting raised and pointed arches.

100 bottom right The magnificent Gothic structure of Sant'Anastasia contains the famous Pisanello fresco St. George Saving The Princess. *This photo shows the interior of the church.*

100-101 San Zeno Maggiore is one of the most magnificent examples of Romanesque architecture in Northern Italy. It was built to house the remains of the Patron Saint of Verona, starting in 1120.

In any case, Saint George is not the patron saint of the city. The ever-surprising Verona sought its saint elsewhere, in Africa, according to tradition, in the dark-skinned Saint Zeno. The church dedicated to St. Zeno is the best example of Romanesque architecture in the whole of northern Italy. In magical Verona a star launched like a meteorite lands unfailingly in the central Piazza Bra every Christmas, causing no damage.

A mixture of history and fantasy is the destiny of Verona, and the legend of two star-crossed lovers, first immortalized by the fertile pen of Luigi da Porto from Vicenza, persuaded two more authors, first Matteo Bandello and then Shakespeare, to write the most heartbreaking and realistic love story of all time. An inn at 27 Via Cappello was transformed long ago into Juliet's house. Standing under its marble balcony, which makes lovers sigh and evokes romantic nocturnal encounters, disturbed only by the song of the unwelcome lark heralding the imminent dawn which ineluctably separates the lovers, the significance of the words pronounced by the handsome Romeo before leaving his beloved town can be clearly understood:

"There is no world without Verona walls,
But purgatory, torture, hell itself.
Hence-banished is banish'd from the world,
And world's exile is death."
(Romeo and Juliet, *Act Three, Scene Three*).

*102 top and bottom
This magnificent part of
Palazzo Giusti in Verona
is a delightful spot full of
greenery, fanciful tree
shapes, and mythological
statues.*

*102 center and 103 One of
the loveliest examples of an
Italian-style Renaissance
garden, with pergolas,
fountains, and viewpoints,
can be admired at Palazzo
Giusti in Verona.*

104-105 Verona by night offers some lovely views of **palazzi** *and monuments overlooking the River Adige.*

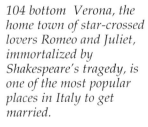

104 bottom Verona, the home town of star-crossed lovers Romeo and Juliet, immortalized by Shakespeare's tragedy, is one of the most popular places in Italy to get married.

105 left The Gothic complex of Sant'Anastasia and the Lamberti Tower dominate the city once ruled by the La Scala family in this lovely night view.

105 right The Madonna Verona fountain, based on a Roman statue that was moved to the center of Piazza delle Erbe in 1368, has become a symbol of the city over the centuries.

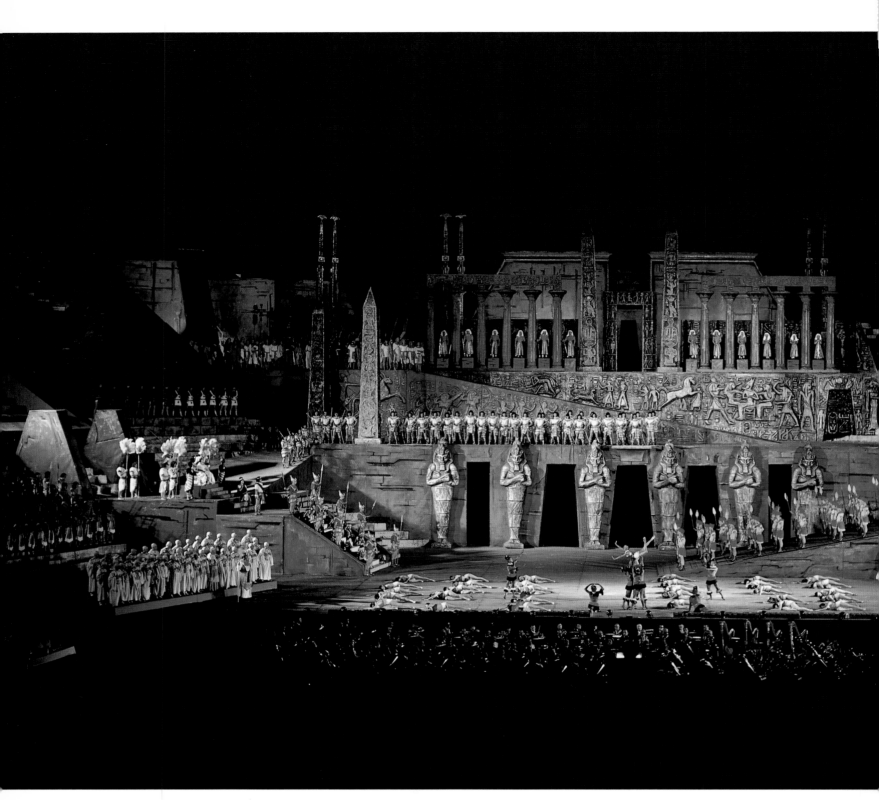

106-107 *Thanks to the magical Arena, one of the few functioning open-air opera theaters in the world, the Verona operatic season attracts a regular crowd of opera lovers every summer.*

106 bottom There is no better venue for Verdi's *Aida, with its sumptuous sets, triumphal march, and superb choreography, than the huge stage of the Verona Arena.*

107 top and bottom The huge elliptical amphitheater, which dominates Piazza Bra, was built in the first century A.D. for gladiator fights, indicating the importance of Verona in Roman times.

107 center The first season of the Opera Festival, to which Verona's Arena owes its fame, opened on August 10, 1913.

Verona holds more surprises for lovers of nature and the best produce. Soave is a town that truly lives up to its name which means "delightful." Perhaps it was a connoisseur who bestowed this name on the town, who fell in love not only with this peaceful spot (although a fortress and defensive city walls bear witness to a warlike past), but above all with its excellent white wine and the neat vineyards on the hillsides, a potentially more persuasive argument. Excellent vines also abound in the Monti Lessini area, which is a very good place to try Valpolicella. The red marble known as "Verona marble," a highly-prized material of which traces can be seen in many aristocratic buildings all over Veneto, actually comes from Sant'Ambrogio di Valpolicella.

Celebrated in immortal verses from Virgil's Georgics, "Fluctibus et fremitu adsurgens, Benace, marino..." (Benacus... with billowy uproar surging like the main), Lake Garda, was called Benacus by the Romans. It holds many delights in store, such as Peschiera, the site of one of the four ancient fortresses that formed the

famous, fearsome Quadrilateral. From there, on a clear day, the lovely Sirmione peninsula can be seen far off, with the Rocca Scaligera jutting out into the heart of the lake. Sirmione, the birthplace of Catullus, another poet who extolled these lovely spots, lies in Lombardy, because the boundary between the Veneto and Lombardy regions starts here at Peschiera, runs along the lakeside and up across Bardolino and Torri del Benaco to Malcesine, at the foot of Mount Baldo, a town associated with an unpleasant memory described by Goethe in his Italienische Reise.

Goethe was attracted by the castle because of its dominant position jutting out over the sea. It

was wide open, with neither doors nor guards, and he began contentedly drawing the tower and ruins in preparation for a picturesque landscape. Unfortunately, he was mistaken for a spy in the pay of the Emperor of Austria, and forced to explain himself to the mayor and a group of impertinent onlookers. However, the author of Faust was not at all dismayed by this adventure, and his first good impression was soon restored. The undeniable beauty of these shores and those famous verses by Virgil continue to attract visitors, and generation after generation of German tourists have made Malcesine their second home.

108 top The delightful Val di Sogno, a lovely green valley on the Lake Garda road between Cassone and Malcesine, is one of the most popular spots in the area attracting tourists from all over the world.

108 bottom This photo shows the delightful marina of Cassone, a hamlet to the south of Malcesine.

108-109 Baia delle Sirene (Mermaid Bay) at Punta San Vigilio offers one of the most romantic views over Lake Garda.

110-111 Malcesine, the northernmost town in the province of Verona, is a popular resort in summer and winter alike because of its delightful location on the slopes of Mount Baldo.

111 top The real attraction of Malcesine is the castle, perched high above Lake Garda. The keep, which was built in the fourteenth century under the rule of the La Scala family, now houses the city's History Museum.

111 center Malcesine's main source of income is tourism, and the marina, with its famous cafés and hotels, is always crowded with tourists, especially Germans following in the footsteps of Goethe.

111 bottom A cable car, from which breathtaking views can be seen, takes visitors rapidly from the town of Malcesine to Tratto Spino, at an altitude of 5900 feet.

THE DOLOMITES AND THE BELLUNO DISTRICT

112 top The medieval town of Feltre, perched high on a hill, relives its glorious past during the annual Palio (tournament), when residents take part in archery contests and horse races.

112 bottom Auronzo di Cadore, dominated by magnificent Dolomite scenery, is one of the most famous mountain resorts, and one of the greatest attractions of the area is the small lake of Santa Caterina, a long reservoir closed by a dam.

112-113 Belluno, attractively encircled by mountains, looks down on the confluence of the Rivers Ardo and Piave, and constitutes the gateway to the Veneto Dolomites.

We have just left Vittorio Veneto, the furthermost outpost of the Province of Treviso. When the city was formed in 1866 by the merger of two delightful towns, Céneda and Serravalle, it inherited its unimaginative name from Vittorio Emanuele II, then King of Italy, but it is better known for the battle that ended World War I in 1918. Now, we set off on the last stage of our journey across Veneto to visit the famous mountains of the Belluno district.

One place definitely worth a visit is the attractive town of Feltre, which occupies the southernmost part of the Belluno Valley. Rich in art and history, it is also known as the "painted town" because the façades of many of its sixteenth-century palazzi are decorated with colorful frescoes. The façade of the Diocesan Curia portrays the Battle of Lepanto, while Palazzo della Ragione, with its porticoed loggia, was built to a design by Andrea Palladio. The town is proud of its close ties with Venice, as demonstrated by the traditional pageant held on the first Sunday of August to commemorate its annexation to the Republic of Venice in 1404. During this festival, Feltre relives its glorious past amid knights, ladies, and squires in traditional costume, the sound of trumpets and drums, and a horse race in which riders representing the "four quarters" of the town compete for a purse of 15 gold ducats. This loyalty is still repaid even today by the regular presence of partygoers from Venice, even though the town is known for its very changeable climate.

Nearby Belluno, "Queen of the Piave," is also known as "shining city" according to a dubious Celtic etymology. The capital of the Dolomites stands in a magnificent position, with a tiara of mountains to the north (Mount Serva, Mount Pelf, and the "Bishop's Needle"), the rocky pyramid of Mount Pizzocco to the west, and Mount Nevegal to the south. The confluence of the tortuous, foaming River Piave with the smaller Ardo encircles and embellishes the center

113 top Nineteenth-century scientist and author Antonio Stoppani used this apt metaphor to describe the enchanting Agordo basin: "Just imagine you're in the middle of the serrated circle of a huge king's crown."

of Belluno, a small, welcoming town with a less frenetic pace of life than most Veneto towns. Like the others, however, it retains the typical, original layout of the streets and porticoes, which can be seen between Piazza dei Martiri, the central shopping area, where the locals promenade up and down, and Piazza Duomo, the monumental center of the city, with its cathedral, designed by Tullio Lombardo, and the Civic Tower, which recalls the time long ago when the city was ruled by count-bishops. However, Piazza Duomo is dominated by the unusual façade of Palazzo dei Rettori, with its twin mullioned windows and columns recalling the Venetian world, an impression that is reinforced by the clock tower which so ostentatiously resembles the Moorish Clock Tower in St. Mark's Square. True human warmth and some delightful sights are also to be found in the picturesque Piazza del Mercato, with the lovely fountain of San Lucano, the Renaissance palazzi, Loggia de' Ghibellini and the Monte di Pietà (pawnbrokers') building.

Leaving Belluno, in Pieve di Cadore, the birthplace of Titian, the artist's simple wooden house with its typical outer gallery facing the sun has been turned into a museum displaying relics of the artist's life. Titian transferred the delights and lovely colors of that sky to his canvases. As a child, he absorbed its colors and then expressed them through the magic of his art so that they can be shared and enjoyed by all. The people of Cadore are tough folk, used to hard work and sacrifice. After being ruled by the Lords of Camino and the Counts of the Tyrol, they voted to merge with the Republic of Venice to the cry of Eamus Ad Bonos Venetos (Let's join the good people of Venice!).

The first fundamental by-laws for the protection of the woods, the main source of wealth of the whole Cadore community, were passed here at Pieve. "Saint Mark's Wood" was vitally important to Venice, but the availability of timber obviously depended mainly on the possibility of transporting it easily, so the logs were cut down to a convenient size, floated down the Piave and Boite rivers as far as possible, then loaded onto rafts and towed to Venice.

These districts are now famous for another type of product, and a modern building on the road leading from Pieve to the nearby Tai di Cadore houses the Eyeglass Museum. The museum's interesting collection, which comprises over 2000 pairs of spectacles dating from the Middle Ages to the present day, reconstructs the fascinating history of what was originally a

114-115 San Pietro di Cadore, which stands amid conifer woods, was one of the main suppliers of wood to the Venetian Republic in days of old.

115 bottom One of the most famous sons of Pieve, capital of Cadore, was Titian, whose humble birthplace now houses a museum featuring the life and works of the great artist.

116-117 Mount Pelmo,
nicknamed "the Cart of the
Almighty" because of its
truncated cone shape,
introduces new arrivals
from the plains to the world
of the Dolomites with its
imperious presence.

116 bottom Santa Fosca is
a pretty mountain resort
nestling in Val Fiorentina,
an oasis of greenery.

117 top *The source of the River Piave is on Mount Peralba, at the head of Val Visdende. Before it was diverted, the river flowed into the Venice lagoon after following a long route, carrying valuable loads of timber for the Venetian Republic.*

117 bottom *Mount Civetta is inextricably linked with the history of the sixth grade on the mountaineering scale of difficulty. Visitors to Alleghe are sure to admire the North-West Face, whose owl shape gives the mountain its name.*

simple trade, but has developed in these mountain areas to a highly profitable business whose products are renowned all over the world.

However, the real asset and the true beauty of the Belluno district is to be found in the mountains. The Dolomites, a wonderful natural amphitheater that emerged from the sea and was forged by the elements, are named after a globe-trotting geologist with the resounding name of Déodat-Guy-Sylvain-Tancrède de Gratet de Dolomieu (1750-1801), who was the first to study the sedimentary rocks collected in these mountains and to discover their unusual composition based on a mineral, never previously classified, which is a double carbonate of calcium and magnesium. However, if the scientist is forgiving, the legendary name of "Pale Mountains" is perhaps preferable and much more fitting to the eminently human characteristic of these mountains, with their pale color and the phenomenon that causes them to turn slowly from pink to deep purple at sunset. This spectacle

of nature is called *enrosadira* in the Engadine dialect, and the term is also to be found in the most authoritative Italian dictionaries.

The air is pure and rarefied, rendered mild even at the coldest times of winter by the gentle warmth of the sun which peeps into the magnificent Ampezzo valley that contains the exclusive holiday resort of Cortina, "pearl of the Dolomites." The spectacular charm of its magnificent surroundings, constituted by Mounts Tofane, Cristallo, Sorapis, Pomagagnon, Croda da Lago, and Nuvolau, to name but a few, makes it truly unique. A resort popular with VIPs, business magnates, and show business personalities, it is becoming increasingly inaccessible because of its prohibitive, ever-

122 top A great attraction for ice climbers following Via dei Finanzieri is Punta Rocca, the largest glacier in the Dolomites, although it is rapidly receding, or Punta Penia on the North Face.

122 bottom This mountain range, The Pale di San Martino, marks the border between Trentino and Veneto. The last part of Cime di Focobon is situated on the Veneto side of the regional border.

123 "I'm made of stone and never move/I'm made of rock and freeze at night/I'm a lonely girl and I don't know why." This is how a Belluno folk song describes the magnificent group of Mount Marmolada, the Queen of the Dolomites.

124-125 The Pale di San Martino constitute the easternmost mountain range in Trentino, on the Veneto border. These magnificent peaks, which are snow-capped all year round, were beloved of Belluno writer Dino Buzzati.

increasing prices. Sightseers who visit the resort at great expense stroll along Corso Italia, the meeting-place of Cortina's glitterati, hoping to see the stars. This ritual promenade is called the struscio (shuffle), because people are liable to wear their shoes out this way. All that remains of the ancient Ampezzo families is a pale recollection in the occasional coat of arms still decorating the façades of the oldest houses or the former Town Hall. The glorious days when blissful peace and quiet could be enjoyed here, far from the traffic, are long gone.

Those were the days of the first famous "Ampezzo Squirrels," the group of climbers inspired by legendary Viennese mountaineer Paul Grohmann, who first started climbing in the Dolomites. His many outstanding followers not only had incredible stamina but also a deep love for the mountains, and never forgot that indescribable sensations must always be accompanied by experience if beauty is not to be paid for with human lives, whereas nowadays, all too many people believe themselves to be experienced guides and tackle the mountains with futuristic equipment, yet lacking the necessary skills.

However, visitors to the Dolomites can satisfy their appetite for nature without risking their skin. Breathtaking views and chocolate-box pictures are imprinted on the waters of Lakes Auronzo and Misurina, which reflect the snow-capped peaks of Mount Cristallino and the Marmarole, the impressive Three Peaks of Lavaredo, and the enchanting, variegated vegetation of the dark woods. Rather like Narcissus, this world is enchanted by its own beauty. The landscape changes: silent hollows alternate with impenetrable thickets where it is easy to imagine that gnomes and elves still dance or play hide-and-seek in the dark cavities of the trees, and watch, silent and ecstatic, the sudden appearance of an acrobatic chamois deer that trots nonchalantly along an inaccessible ledge, or a golden eagle with its menacing shadow plummeting down from the heights where it has built its nest onto some small creature that vainly seeks to escape, while majestic deer graze undisturbed with aristocratic slowness in the Belluno Dolomites National Park. Here, man has learned to listen to silence, to rejoice in the sacred slow passage of time, and to understand that true civilization has an ancient, primitive soul, very different from the "false, lying gods" of our so-called progress.

126-127 *Terza Grande, Clap Grande, and Mount Siera, which encircle Sappada, make a very interesting nature trek. The names of these little-known groups are influenced by the dialect of nearby Friuli.*

127 top *Cima Piccola, Cima Grande, and Cima Ovest constitute the main part of one of the best-known groups in the Dolomites, the Three Peaks of Lavaredo, which climbers call the "Fantastic Trinity."*

127 center *This photo shows the characteristic haylofts called* tabià, *which have been part of the mountain landscape of Veneto since time immemorial, with the snow-capped Mount Pelmo in the background.*

127 left *Torre del Barancio, Lusy, Romana, Grande, Terza, Quarta, and Inglese are the names of the "Five Towers" (although there are actually more than five peaks, as shown by their names). The highest stands at 525 feet, and they are used as a training ground by the famous mountaineering club called the Cortina Squirrels.*

TRADES AND TRADITIONS

The importance of ancient trades is easy to understand in the Veneto region. Just the fact that Venice, its capital, is a manmade city would have been incomprehensible, and above all impossible, without the work of a host of tradesmen. Secrets jealously preserved for centuries have been handed down from father to son through generations of tradesmen, some from the Italian mainland. What would Venice be without its stone-masons, without the smiths who tame fire like the divine Hephaestus, and without the skilled carpenters who carve the sinuous shapes and knots of no less than eight types of wood into elegant, asymmetrical gondolas in their boatyards? Could the magnificent furnishings of the palazzi overlooking the Grand Canal have survived over the centuries without a thriving community of stucco workers, varnishers, wood-carvers, and gilders? Could Murano exist without glass?

Humble sand containing silica, combined with lime and soda which helps it to melt, is transformed in the furnace into an incandescent substance that seems to capture rays of sunlight or harness the glimmerings of twilight in a shapeless blob to which the rapid, skillful gestures of the master glassmaker give body and life. A few deft moves with the pliers, and the structure reveals its soul and releases its colors. The metamorphosis of matter takes place before our astonished gaze: slender,

128 top Gondola construction still follows ancient rules. No less than eight kinds of wood are needed for the body parts and finishing: fir, larch, cherry, walnut, elm, sessile oak, linden, and mahogany.

128 center and bottom The Venetian word squero means the shipyard where gondolas are still built. It derives from squadra (set square), the tool still used by carpenters to make them.

128-129 According to tradition, the tall stem of the gondola symbolizes the curve of the Grand Canal, the six points at the front symbolize the six neighborhoods into which Venice is divided, and the one at the back symbolizes La Giudecca.

129 bottom The forcola (rowlock), which is fitted into a special housing on the gondola, is made of a single piece of walnut burr and finished like a veritable woodcarving.

bright, colored, transparent glass is born in all its lightness, symbolizing the fragility of the city that invented this art. Lace has the same fragility. According to legend, it incorporates the characteristic lightness of sea foam, raised up on the tail of a generous mermaid as a wedding present for a bridegroom who resisted her lures. You have to see for yourself the incredible motions of an elderly lacemaker in Burano to realize how seemingly clumsy old hands can move with truly unbelievable agility and unravel a complex web of what does indeed appear to be seaweed and sea foam. These older ladies are the only repositories of a complex body of knowledge, and they are capable of producing infinite variations, forming intricate patterns as they wish.

Mask-making was once so common that there was actually a mask-makers' guild in Venice. Masks were introduced into Venice after the conquest of the Levant, and soon they were all the rage, becoming an essential accessory even for the nobility. They were worn for almost 6 months of the year, at times fixed by the rigid Venetian ceremonial

calendar, giving strangers to the city the impression of a delightful, endless carnival. The trade was recently revived to recreate the magic of carnival time. People put on a new face to forget, a new skin to rejuvenate themselves, a new screen of paper mâché to conceal their desires and weaknesses from prying. Venice is not the only city in Veneto with similar craft traditions. Ancient trades such as pottery making are also to be found on the mainland. At Bassano del Grappa, in the magnificent setting of Palazzo Sturm,

130 A full-scale industry has grown up to produce paper mâché masks with creative and grotesque shapes since the Venice Carnival was revived in 1980.

130-131 The craft of wood gilding is still carried on by some small cottage industries in Venice, especially in the construction and restoration of antique picture frames and small carvings.

131 top There are some great masters of woodcarving in Veneto, especially in the mountains, but this craft is no longer quite so genuine as it once was, because its practitioners mainly cater to the tourist market.

131 bottom The resounding forge of Vulcan has some outstanding imitators in Veneto, the home of the last great masters of wrought iron descended from the Bellotto and Rizzarda dynasties and also sculptor Toni Benetton.

132 *The Coppa Barovier, a masterpiece of Murano glass dating from the late 15th century, is one of the most outstanding examples of enamel painting on glass.*

overlooking the River Brenta just a stone's throw from the famous bridge, visitors can see the development of this craft across the ages, from the magnificent eighteenth-century Manardi and Antonibon ceramics made at Nove di Bassano to recent contemporary creations designed by artists of international repute. It is a pity that pottery is commonly known as a "poor man's art form," because the expression does not do justice to the wealth of imagination and creativity that adds quality and artistic beauty to this simple raw material.

The same applies to the mountain tradition of woodworking and woodcarving, both of which are very common in the Belluno area, where artists of the caliber of Augusto Murer of Falcade have numerous disciples. In the field of wrought iron Veneto has also produced masters of Art Nouveau like Umberto Bellotto of Venice and Carlo Rizzarda of Feltre and, more recently, Toni Benetton of Treviso, who have raised the blacksmith's trade to the level of an art. Wealth and luxury are the province of more

noble materials like gold and silver, and the jewelers of present-day Vicenza could easily have amazed the noble ladies of ancient Versailles with their refined tastes.

Veneto means tradition: true, sincere folk traditions, not just shows put on for the benefit of tourists like the Venice Carnival, which was revived in 1980 after an absence of nearly two centuries, much changed from its historical predecessor. Once, the Venetians wore attractive masks to conceal their identity, but nowadays, in the consumer society, those who wear masks and costumes do so merely to show off at a huge party held in the delightful showplace of Venice. To rediscover the healthy

133 left The art of producing decorative blown glass with colored pastes, aventurine, milk-scab, and murrine (tiny colored glass cylinders) has been perfected over the centuries in Murano, and a crucial contribution to the craft has been made by famous designers and some of the leading artists of the 20th century.

133 top right Burano is particularly famous for the type of needle lace known as punto in aria, in which only needle and thread are used, without any background fabric.

133 bottom right The art of ceramic making is widespread in the Vicenza area, and exhibitions are regularly held at the attractive Palazzo Sturm in Bassano to keep the tradition alive.

134-135 It's traditional to dress up at Carnival time in Venice, but the city's residents do so less and less often, because the city is invaded by tourists vying to outdo one another in their colorful costumes.

134 bottom and 135 bottom right Until the Venice Carnival was revived about 20 years ago to encourage tourism to return in what had been the low season, the tradition had remained dormant for centuries.

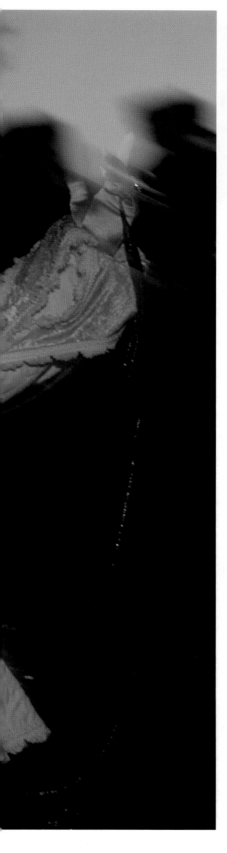

enthusiasm of long ago you have to look elsewhere, at events like the Regatta or the Vogalonga boat race, when traditional craft rowing down the meandering Grand Canal or through the quivering reaches of the lagoon can be admired in a more or less competitive spirit, or at the Chiesa del Redentore, under a hail of fireworks that illuminate the night as bright as day amid a swarm of bobbing boats. Every nose is turned skywards, and cries of joy or criticisms are uttered by the last real Venetians, now relegated to the role of extras in a city that has sold its soul to the tourists.

The joyful revelry of the ancient popular festivals is still to be found in Veneto in the rustic "bread and wine" festivals held on the eve of Epiphany around huge bonfires made from massive piles of wood and stubble to celebrate two of the most important products of the harvest. The direction taken by the sparks of the bonfire is interpreted as an auspicious sign or, much more rarely, as a warning of lean years to come. Over a glass of mulled wine and the auspicious songs of the occasion, the spirits take care not to disturb the atmosphere of merrymaking, because the old-fashioned Veneto recipe for good health and good cheer (rather more nourishing than "an apple a day keeps the doctor away") is still applicable today: "Wear your hat, eat chicken pills, drink wine, and send the doctors off to have a good time."

135 top left and top right One of the greatest amusements for tourists is to pose for hours in front of the most famous monuments in Venice, hoping that a famous cameraman will immortalize the most unusual costumes.

136 The Wake of the Redeemer, held on the third Saturday in July, is one of the most popular festivals with Venetians. This ancient tradition derives from the celebrations held to mark the end of the terrible plague of 1576.

136-137 The Lion of St. Mark on the quay is silhouetted against the sky, while colorful fireworks are set off from the rafts floating on the Giudecca canal at the traditional Redeemer festival.

137 bottom A firework display held in St. Mark's Basin is watched by the whole population of Venice with their traditional boats, decorated for the occasion with tree branches and colored lamps.

139 top and center
The Historic Regatta, which
originated in the Middle
Ages, although the present
version only dates from
1899, is held in Venice on
the first Sunday in
September.

138 bottom and 139 bottom
right The typical regatta
boats are the gondola and
the fast gondolino,
followed by the caorlina,
a lagoon cargo boat, the
pupparino, named after
the streamlined shape of
the poop, the sandolo, a
fishing and pleasure raft,
and its close relative the
mascareta.

139 top and center
The Historic Regatta, which
originated in the Middle
Ages, although the present
version only dates from
1899, is held in Venice on
the first Sunday in
September.

The genuine carnival can be seen in
Verona, where it retains its traditional spirit
and there is an atmosphere of spontaneous
collective gaiety, led by the "Father of
Gnocchi," who actually receives his investiture
in the Church of St. Zeno. According to
tradition, that neighborhood was the birthplace
of the generous Tommaso da Vico, a benefactor
who provided plenty of bread, flour, butter,
wine, and cheese to make gnocchi for
distribution to the hungry populace during the
famine of 1530. The "Father of Gnocchi," an
extravagant character with a white or multicolored suit and a bit of a belly, initiates the
"Gnocchi Bacchanalia" on the last Friday
before Lent, brandishing a huge fork with a
gnocco stuck on it.

There are also costume festivals with
historical pageants, the best-known of which is
held in conjunction with Venice's historic
Regatta on the Grand Canal, when colorful
eight-oared gondolas escort the gondola bearing
the Doge and Caterina Cornaro, Queen of
Cyprus and widow of Lusignano, who donated
her precious kingdom to the Republic of Venice
in 1489, receiving the delightful residence of
Asolo in exchange.

Still in the province of Venice, the Noale
pageant, held at the end of June, features flag
tossers and musicians, and comes to a
spectacular conclusion with the burning of the
tower. The Marciliana pageant, held in

138-139 The Vogalonga
regatta, inaugurated in
1975 to revive the "Veneto-
style rowing" tradition, is
now internationally famous.

138 bottom left One phase
of the non-competitive
Vogalonga regatta
concludes when the crews
row under the Three Arches
bridge crossing the
Cannaregio canal, cheered
on by the crowd.

140 top The historical
pageant commemorates the
return to Venice in 1489 of
Caterina Cornaro, Queen
of Cyprus and widow of
Lusignano, who donated
her precious kingdom to
the Venetian Republic.

140 bottom A procession of
boats called **bissone**, with
their rich, baroque pavilions
and canopies, sails along
the River Brenta during the
September Flower Festival.

Chioggia during the third weekend of June,
commemorates the victory won in 1380, when
the people of Chioggia fought alongside the
Venetians against the Genoese. The pageant,
founded quite recently, but based on detailed
historical research, is named after a
characteristic Chioggia boat and involves three
contests: the archery contest, the scaule race
(scaule are small boats manned by four
oarsmen and two crossbowmen, normally used
to escort noblemen or the mayor), and the
crossbowmen's relay.

Other famous events are the Feltre pageant,
already mentioned, and the equally celebrated
pageant of the ten Montagnana towns,
involving a horse race in which expert jockeys
represent the 10 communities of the ancient
Lombard district of Montagnana. The pageant
has ancient origins: it commemorates the
liberation of the towns from the tyranny of
Ezzelino III da Romano.

The most famous of these enjoyable costume
events is the living chess game played every
two years (in even years) at Marostica on the
second Sunday in September. Back in 1454, the
city was ruled by Mayor Taddeo Parisio, a man
of intellect and, some say, a humanist. Two
proud noblemen, Vieri di Vallonara and
Rinaldo di Angaran, both claimed the hand of

141 The Historic Regatta
in Venice is a very popular
event, and tourists
particularly enjoy the
pageant that precedes
the regatta.

Lionora, his daughter. Finding himself charged, yet again, with ruling on an affair of the heart, he decided to apply to the letter an ancient ordinance which required such questions to be resolved without bloodshed over the chessboard. After a number of moves accompanied by a running commentary from the herald, the goddess of fortune, blind as love, eventually decided in favor of Lionora's favorite, Vieri di Vallonara. However, his adversary was not left empty-handed. As a consolation prize for being check-mated, the mayor gave him the hand of his sister Oldrada, who was less attractive than her young niece. This civilized decision, which left the tricky question to be decided by human ability and intellectual qualities rather than the brute force of the rivals, can teach us something even now.

Now we have played our match, but do not know whether we have won or lost. The stakes were high, but those who defend the colors of Veneto begin with an advantage, and we will leave it up to the reader to judge the outcome.

142 top The streets of Chioggia are filled with period costumes and weapons on the third weekend in June, during the Marciliana pageant held to commemorate the victory of 1380 when Chioggia fought with Venice against Genoa.

142 bottom This photo shows the traditional costume worn by the women of Cortina d'Ampezzo at folk festivals.

142-143 A delightful chess game, held in the mediaeval setting of Marostica, commemorates the rivalry between two gentlemen for the hand of the beautiful madonna Lionora.

143 bottom left This traditional wooden effigy from the Sappada Carnival is supposed to release the ancient spirits

of fertility so that they banish the rigors of winter and reawaken the spring as soon as possible.

143 bottom right The traditional carnival character from Sappada called Rollate is named after the jangling bronze balls tied around his waist which announce his arrival, brandishing a broom, to open the Carnival procession.

144 The gondola, with its sinuously elegant shape, reigns supreme in Venice. It has survived unchanged through the centuries, proving superior to the technological innovations which are so out of place in the calm and silence of the lagoon.

PHOTO CREDITS

Antonio Attini / Archivio White Star : pages 8, 10 top, 80, 81, 82, 83, 90, 90-91, 91 top, 92, 93, 107 bottom, 108 top, 111 - Marcello Bertinetti / Archivio White Star : pages 1, 2-3, 9, 18, 19, 21 bottom, 26, 27, 28, 29, 30 top right, 30 bottom, 32, 33, 34 top, 36 bottom, 37, 42, 43, 44, 45, 46-47, 48, 49 bottom, 50 bottom, 51, 52, 53, 55 top, 119, 122, 123, 124-125, 127 bottom, 128 center and bottom, 128-129, 130, 130-131, 134 bottom, 135 bottom, 136 bottom, 137 bottom, 138, 139, 142 bottom, 144 - Luciano Ramires / Archivio White Star : pages 10 bottom, 62, 63, 113 top, 114, 116, 117, 143 bottom - Giulio Veggi / Archivio White Star : pages 13 right, 68, 69, 71 bottom, 72 bottom, 98, 99 bottom, 100 top left, 102, 103, 104, 105 - Antonio Attini : page 135 top and center - Loris Barbazza : pages 65 top, 128 top, 133 top - Carlo Borlenghi / Sea & See Italia : page 142 top - Cameraphoto : pages 16 center and bottom, 16-17, 17 bottom, 20 bottom, 20-21, 22 top and center, 24 bottom, 24-25, 25, 30 top left, 30 center, 31, 34 bottom, 34-35, 35 bottom, 36-37, 40-41, 41, 48-49, 55 bottom, 56 top left, 56 bottom, 57, 66 top, 70, 70-71, 71 top, 74, 75, 78-79, 100 top and bottom right, 133 bottom left, 136-137, 140 top, 141 - Foto Elio and Stefano Ciol : page 73 - Marco Cristofori / Sie : pages 16 top, 50-51, 54-55, 91 bottom - Gianfranco Fainello / Archivio Fondazione Arena di Verona : pages 106 bottom, 107 top and center - Fantuz / Sime: page 79 bottom - F. Gorup De Besanez : pages 60, 115 bottom, 136 top, 142-143 - Johanna Huber / Sime : pages 21 top, 38 center, 56 top right, 58 center, 64-65, 66-67, 76, 77, 88-89, 94-95, 100-101, 108 bottom, 108-109, 112, 114-115, 118-119, 120-121, 126-127, 127 top and center - Archivio SCALA : pages 22 bottom, 22-23, 66 bottom, 72 top, 86 center, 106-107, 132 - Giovanni Simeone / Sime: pages 4-5, 6-7, 10-11, 12-13, 14-15, 23 bottom, 38 top and bottom, 38-39, 40 bottom, 58-59, 61, 72-73, 84 top, 84-85, 85, 86 top, 97 top, 98-99, 110-111, 112-113, 134-135 - Marc. E. Smith : pages 54 bottom, 58 bottom, 79 top, 82-83, 84 bottom, 87, 96, 97 center, 97 bottom, 100 bottom left, 129 bottom, 131 right, 133 bottom right, 140 bottom.

AIR CONCESSION

Concession S.M.A. 12.121 of 20-09-1994 : pages 16 top, 50-51, 54-55.
Concession S.M.A. 12.178 of 25-091995 : page 60.
Concession S.M.A. 12-180 of 11-11-1994 : pages 16 center and bottom, 16-17, 56 top left.

TRANSLATION: A.B.A., Milan